WINGS AND THE CHILD

This edition published by Lector House in 2024

ISBN: 978-93-6138-179-9

Lector House LLP
Registered Office: H. No. 96, Block C, Tomar Colony,
Burari, Delhi – 110084, India
info@lectorhouse.com
www.lectorhouse.com

WINGS AND THE CHILD

EDITH NESBIT

2024

LECTOR HOUSE

LECTOR HOUSE LLP

Photo David Norris] [*Frontispiece*

Portrait of the Author.

WINGS AND THE CHILD

OR

THE BUILDING OF MAGIC CITIES

BY

E. NESBIT

AUTHOR OF

"THE MAGIC CITY," "THE WOULDBEGOODS," ETC., ETC.

WITH PICTURES BY GEORGE BARRAUD AND FROM PHOTOGRAPHS

TO THE READER

WHEN this book first came to my mind it came as a history and theory of the building of Magic Cities on tables, with bricks and toys and little things such as a child may find and use. But as I kept the thought by me it grew and changed, as thoughts will do, until at last it took shape as an attempt to contribute something, however small and unworthy, to the science of building a magic city in the soul of a child, a city built of all things pure and fine and beautiful. As you read, it will, I hope, seem to you that something of what I say is true—in much, no doubt, it will seem to you that I am mistaken; but however you may disagree with me, you will, I trust, at least have faith in the honesty of my purpose. If I seem to you to be too dogmatic, to lay down the law too much as though I were the teacher and you the learner, I beg you to believe that it is in no such spirit that I have written. Rather it is as though you and I, spending a quiet evening by your fire, talked together of the things that matter, and as though I laid before you all the things that were in my heart—not stopping at every turn to say "Do you not think so too?" and "I hope you agree with me?" but telling you, straight from the heart, what I have felt and thought and, I humbly say, known about children and the needs of children. I have talked to you as to a friend, without the reservations and apologies which we use with strangers. And if, in anything, I shall have offended you, I entreat you to extend to me the forgiveness and the forbearance which you would exercise towards a friend who had offended you, not meaning to offend, and to believe that I have spoken to you as frankly and plainly as I would wish you to speak to me, were you the writer and I the reader.

E. NESBIT.

CONTENTS

LIST OF ILLUSTRATIONS

PART I

CHAPTER I

OF UNDERSTANDING

It is not with any pretension to special knowledge of my subject that I set out to write down what I know about children. I have no special means of knowing anything: I do, in fact, know nothing that cannot be known by any one who will go to the only fount of knowledge, experience. And by experience I do not mean scientific experience, that is the recorded results of experiments, the tabulated knowledge wrung from observation; I mean personal experience, that is to say, memory. You may observe the actions of children and chronicle their sayings, and produce from these, perhaps, a lifelike sketch of a child, as it appears to the grown-up observer; but observation is no key to the inner mysteries of a child's soul. The only key to those mysteries is in knowledge, the knowledge of what you yourself felt when you were good and little and a child. You can remember how things looked to you, and how things looked to the other children who were your intimates. Our own childhood, besides furnishing us with an exhaustless store of enlightening memories, furnishes us with the one opportunity of our lives for the observation of children—other children. There is a freemasonry between children, a spontaneous confidence and give-and-take which is and must be for ever impossible between children and grown-ups, no matter how sympathetic the grown-up, how confiding the child. Between the child and the grown-up there is a great gulf fixed—and this gulf, the gulf between one generation and another, can never be really bridged. You may learn to see across it, a little, or sometimes in rare cases to lean very far across it so that you can just touch the tips of the little fingers held out from the other side. But if your dealings with those on the other side of the gulf are to be just, generous, noble, and helpful, they must be motived and coloured by your memories of the time when you yourself were on the other side—when you were a child full of your own hopes, dreams, aims, interests, instincts, and imaginings, and over against you, kindly perhaps, tenderly loving, often tenderly loved, but still in some mysterious way antagonistic and counting as "Them," were the grown-ups. I might say elders, parents, teachers, spiritual pastors and masters, but the word which the child himself uses seems to me, for all reasons, to be the best word for my use, because it expresses fully and finally the nature of the gulf between. The grown-ups are the people who once were children and who have forgotten what it felt like to be a child. And Time marks with the same outward brand those who have forgotten and those who do not forget. So that even the few who have managed to slip past the Customs-house with their bundle of memories intact can never fully display them. These are a sort of contraband, and neither the children nor the grown-ups will ever believe that that which we have brought with us from the land of childhood is genuine. The grown-ups accuse us of invention, sometimes praise us for it, when all we have is memory; and the children imagine that we must have been watching them, and thus surprised a few of their secrets, when all that we have is the secrets which were our own when we were children—secrets which were so bound up with the fibre of our nature that we could never lose them, and so go through life with them, our dearest treasures. Such people feel to the end that they are children in a grown-up world. For a middle-aged gentleman with a beard or a stout elderly lady with spectacles to move among other elderly and spectacled persons feeling that they are still children, and that the other elderly and spectacled ones are really grown-ups, seems thoroughly unreasonable, and therefore those who have never forgotten do not, as a rule, say anything about it. They just mingle with the other people, looking as grown-up as any one—but in their hearts they are only pretending to be grown-up: it is like acting in a charade. Time with his make-up box of lines and wrinkles, his skilful brush that paints out the tints and the contours of youth, his supply of grey wigs and rounded shoulders and pillows for the waist, disguises the actors well enough, and they go through life altogether unsuspected. The tired eyes close on a world which to them has always been the child's world, the tired hands loose the earthly possessions which have, to them, been ever the toys of the child. And deep in their hearts is the faith and the hope that in the life to come it may not be necessary to pretend to be grown-up.

Such people as these are never pessimists, though they may be sinners; and they will be trusting, to the verge of what a real grown-up would call imbecility. To them the world will be, from first to last, a beautiful place, and every unbeautiful thing will be a surprise, hurting them like a sudden blow. They will never learn prudence, or parsimony, nor know, with the unerring instinct of the really grown-up, the things that are or are not done by the best people. All their lives they will love, and expect love—and be sad, wondering helplessly when they do not get it. They will expect beautiful quixotic impulsive generosities and splendours from a grown-up world which has forgotten what impulse was: and to the very end they will not leave off expecting. They will be easily pleased and easily hurt, and the grown-ups in grain will contemplate their pains and their pleasures with an uncomprehending irritation.

If these children, disguised by grown-up bodies, are ever recognised for what they are, it is when they happen to have the use of their pens—when they write for and about children. Then grown-up people will call them intelligent and observant, and children will write to them and ask the heart-warm, heart-warming question, "How did you know?" For if they can become articulate they will speak the language that children understand, and children will love, not them, for their identity is cloaked with grey grown-up-ness, but what they say. There are some of these in whom the fire of genius burns up and licks away the trappings under which Time seeks to disguise them—Andersen, Stevenson, Juliana Ewing were such as these—and the world knows them for what they were, and adores in them what in the uninspired it would decry and despise.

The King's Summer-House.

To these others who have the memories of childhood untainted and yet have not the gift and relief of words, to these I address myself in the first instance, because they will understand without any involved explanation on my part what it is that I am driving at, and it is these who, alone, can teach the real grown-ups the things which they have forgotten. For these things can be taught, these things can be re-learned. I would have every man and woman in whom the heart of childhood still lives, protest, however feebly and haltingly, yet with all the power of the heart, against machine-made education—against the instruction which crams a child with facts and starves it of dreams, which forces the free foot into heavy boots and bids it walk on narrow pavement, which crushes with heavy hand the wings of the soul, and presses the flower of imagination flat between the pages of a lexicon.

CHAPTER II

NEW WAYS

"WHAT," we ask with anxious gravity, "what is the best sort of teaching for children?" One might as sanely ask what is the best sort of spectacles for men, or the best size in gloves for women. And the blind coarse generalisation which underlies that question is the very heart and core of the muddled, musty maze we call education. We talk of the best sort of education for children, as we might talk of the best sort of polish for stoves, the best sort of nourishment for mice. Stoves are all alike, they vary in ugliness perhaps, but the iron soul of one is as the iron soul of the other. The polish that is good for one is good for all. Mice may, and do, vary in size and colour; their mousehood does not vary, nor their taste for cheese. In the inner nature, in the soul and self of it, each child is different from any other child, and the education that treats children as a class and not as individual human beings is the education whose failure is bringing our civilisation about our ears even as we speak.

Each child is an explorer in a new country—an explorer with its own special needs and curiosities. We put up iron railings to keep the explorers to our own sordidly asphalted paths. The little free wild creatures would seek their meat from God: we round them into herds, pen them in folds, and feed them with artificial foods—drab flat oil cakes all alike, not considering that for some brown nuts and red berries, and for some the new clean green grass, may be the bread of life.

Or, if you take the mind of a child to be a garden wherein flowers grow that might be trained to beauty, you bring along your steam-roller, and crush everything to a flat field where you may grow cabbages. It is so good for the field, you say—because you like cabbages.

Liberty is one of the rights we claim for ourselves, though God knows we get little enough of it and use still less; and Liberty is one of the rights that a child above all needs—every possible liberty, of thought, of word, of deed. The old systems of education seem to have found it good to coerce a child for the simple sake of coercion—to make it do what the master chose, to make it leave undone those things which it wished to do and to do those things which it did not wish to do—nay, more, wished violently and conclusively not to do. To force the choice of the teacher on the child, to override the timid natural impulses of the child with the hard hoofs of the teacher's individuality, to crush out all initiative, to force the young supple mind into a mould, to lop the budding branches, nip off the sensitive seeking tendrils, to batter down the child's will by the brute force of the grown-up will, to "break the child's spirit," as the cursed phrase used to run—this was, in effect, what education meant. There was a picture in *Punch*, I remember—at least I have forgotten the picture, but I remember the legend: "Cissy, go and see what Bobbie's doing, and tell him not to."

It did not much matter what you made a child do, so long as it was something against the grain. He was to learn, not what he with his wonderful new curiosities and aptitudes longed to learn, but what you wished to teach; you with your dulled senses—dulled in the same bitter school as that in which he was now a sad learner.

Not much Higher than the Table.

Generation after generation has gone on, pounding away at the old silly game, each generation anxious and eager to hurt the new one as it, in its time, was hurt. Each generation must, one would have thought, have remembered what things hurt children and how much these things hurt, and yet this intolerable cycle of bullying and punishment and repression went on and on and on. Children were bullied and broken—and grew up to bully and break in their turn. It must be that this was because the grown-ups did not remember. Those who have the care of children, who work for them, who teach them, should be those who do remember: those who have not forgotten what it feels like to be a child—any sort of child. For, though children are all different, there is a common measure among them as there is among men. A law for men cannot be good if it be made—as indeed but too often happens—by those who have forgotten what it used to feel like to be a man; and what sort of poetry do you get from one who has forgotten beauty and sorrow, and the Spring, and how it feels to be young and a lover? And if the people who have the care of children have forgotten what it feels like to be a child, those who do remember should remind them. They should be reminded how it feels to be not so very much higher than the table, how it feels not to be so clever as you are now, and so much more interested in so much more—how it feels to believe in things and in people as you did when you were new to the journey of life—to explore every road you came to, to trust every person you met. It is a long time ago, but can you not remember the days when right and wrong were as different as milk and mud, when you knew that it was really wrong to be naughty and really good to be good, when you felt that your mother could do no wrong and that your father was the noblest and bravest of men? Do you remember the world of small and new and joyous and delightful things? Try to remember it if you would know how to help a child instead of hindering it—try to look at the world with the clear, clean eyes that once were yours in the days when you had never read a newspaper or deceived a friend. You will then be able to see again certain ideals, unclouded and radiant, which the dust of the crowded highway and the smears of getting-on have dimmed and distorted—quite simple ideals of love, faith, unselfishness, honour, truth. I know these words are often enough on the lips of all of us, but a child's ear will be able to tell whether the words spring from the lips or the heart. Look back, and you will see that you yourself were also able to distinguish these things—once.

Education as it should be, the unfolding of a flower, not the distorting of it, is only possible to those who are willing and able themselves to become as little children.

It is because certain great spirits have done this and have tried to teach others to do it, that reforms in education have begun to be at least possible. Froebel, Pestalozzi, Signora Montessori and many a lesser star has shone upon a new path. And public interest has centred more and more on the welfare of the child. Books are written, societies formed, newspapers founded in the interests of the child, and true education becomes a possibility.

And well indeed it is for us that this is so. For the education of the last three hundred years has led, in all things vital and spiritual, downhill all the way. We have gone on frustrating natural human intelligences and emotions, inculcating false doctrines, and choking with incoherent facts the souls which asked to be fed with dreams-come-true—till now our civilisation is a thing we cannot look at without a mental and moral nausea. We have, in our countrysides, peasants too broken for rebellion, in our cities.

The mortal sickness of a mind
Too unhappy to be kind.

If ever we are to be able to look ourselves and each other in the face again it will be because a new generation has arisen in whose ears the voice of God and His angels has not ceased to sound. If only we would see the things that belong to our peace, and lead the children instead of driving them, who knows what splendid thoughts and actions they in their natural development might bring to the salvation of the world?

In the Palace of Education which the great minds have designed and are designing, many stones will be needed—and so I bring the little stone I have hewn out and tried to shape, in the hope that it may fit into a corner of that great edifice. For if anything is to be done, it is necessary that all who have anything to give, shall give it. As Francis Bacon said:

"Nothing can so much conduce to the drawing down, as it were, from heaven a whole shower of new and profitable Inventions, as this, that the experiments of many ... may come to the knowledge of one man, or some few, who by mutual conference may whet and sharpen one another, so that by this ... Arts may flourish, and as it were by a commixture and communication of Rays, inflame one another.... This sagacity by literate experience may in the mean project and scatter for the benefit of man many rudiments to knowledge which may be had at hand."

And that is why I have left for a little while the telling of stories and set myself to write down something of what I know about children—know by the grace of memory and by the dreams of childhood, to me, thank God, persistent and imperishable.

CHAPTER III

PLAYTHINGS

The prime instinct of a child at play—I do not mean a child at games—is to create. I use the word confidently. He will make as well as create, if you let him, but always he will create: he will use the whole force of dream and fancy to create something out of nothing—over and beyond what he will make out of such materials as he has to hand. The five-year-old will lay a dozen wooden bricks and four cotton reels together, set a broken cup on the top of them, and tell you it is a steam-engine. And it is. He has created the engine which he sees, and you don't see, and the pile of bricks and cotton reels is the symbol of his creation. He will silently borrow your best scissors and cut a serrated band of newspaper, which he will fasten round his head (with your best brooch, if he cannot find a pin), hang another newspaper from his shoulders, and sit in state holding the hearth-brush. He will tell you that he is a king—and he is. He has created crown, robes, sceptre, and kingship. The paper and the rest of it are but symbols.

He has Created the Engine.

The Tomb in the Desert.

And you shall observe that the toys which the child loves best are always those toys which lend themselves to such symbolic use.

Christmas is at hand. You go to buy gifts for the child, in memory of that Other Child whose birthday gifts were gold, frankincense, and myrrh. You go into the toyshops, elbowing your way as best you can, looking for such toys as may aid the child in his work of creative imagination.

You find a vast mass and litter and jumble of incredible futilities—things made to sell, things made by people who have forgotten what it is like to be a child. Mechanical toys of all sorts, stupid toys, toys that will only do one thing, and that thing vulgar and foolish. And, worst outrage of all, ugly toys, monstrosities, deformities, lead devils, grinning humpbacked clowns, "comic" dogs and cats, hideous mis-shapen pigs, incredible negroes, intolerable golliwogs. All such things the natural child, with a child's decent detestation of deformity, will thrust from it with screams of fear and hatred, till the materialistic mother or nurse explains that the horror is not really, as the child knows it to be, horrible and unnatural, but "funny." Thus do we outrage the child's inborn sense of beauty, which is also the sense of health and fitness, and teach it that deformity is not shocking, not pitiable even, but just "funny." All these ugly toys are impossible as aids to clean imagination.

So, almost in as great, though not in so harmful a degree, is the "character doll." The old doll was a doll, and not a character. Therefore she could assume any character at your choice. The character doll is Baby Willy, and can never be anything else, unless imagination, exasperated and baffled, christens him Silly Billy in the moment of furious projection across the nursery floor. But the old doll, with her good, expressionless face and clear blue eyes, could be a duchess or a dairymaid, a captive princess or a greengrocer's wife keeping shop, a cruel stepmother or Joan of Arc. I beg you to try Baby Willy in the character of Joan of Arc.

You cannot hope to understand children by common-sense, by reason, by logic, nor by any science whatsoever. You cannot understand them by imagination—not even by love itself. There is only one way: to remember what you thought and felt and liked and hated when you yourself were a child. Not what you know now—or think you know—you ought to have thought and liked, but what you did then, in stark fact, like and think. There is no other way.

Do you remember the toys you liked, the toys you played with? Do you remember the toys you hated—after the fading of the first day's flush of novelty, of possession? The houses with doors that wouldn't open? The stables with horses that wouldn't stand up? The shops whose goods were part of their painted shelves, whose shopmen were as fast glued behind the counter as any live shop-assistant before the passing of the Shops Act?

And the mechanical toys—the clockwork toys. The engine was all right, even after the clockwork ran down for the last time with that inexorable whizz which told you all was over; you could build tunnels with the big brown books in the library and push the engine through with your hand—it would run quite a long way out on the other side. But the other clockwork things! How can one love and pet a mouse, no matter how furry its superficial exterior, when underneath, where its soft waistcoat and its little feet should be, there is only a hard surface from which incompetent wheels protrude? And the ostrich who draws a hansom cab, and the man who beats the boy with a stick? When they have whizzed their last, who cares for the tin relics outliving their detestable activities?

Think of the toys you liked: the Noah's Ark—full of characters. What stirring dramas of the chase, what sporting incidents, what domestic and agricultural operations could be carried out with that most royal of toys. Mr. Noah, I remember, was equally competent and convincing as ploughman or carter. But his chief rôle was Sitting Bull. His sons were inimitable as Chingachgook and scalp hunters generally. You cannot play scalp hunters with the mechanical ostrich indissolubly welded to a hansom cab.

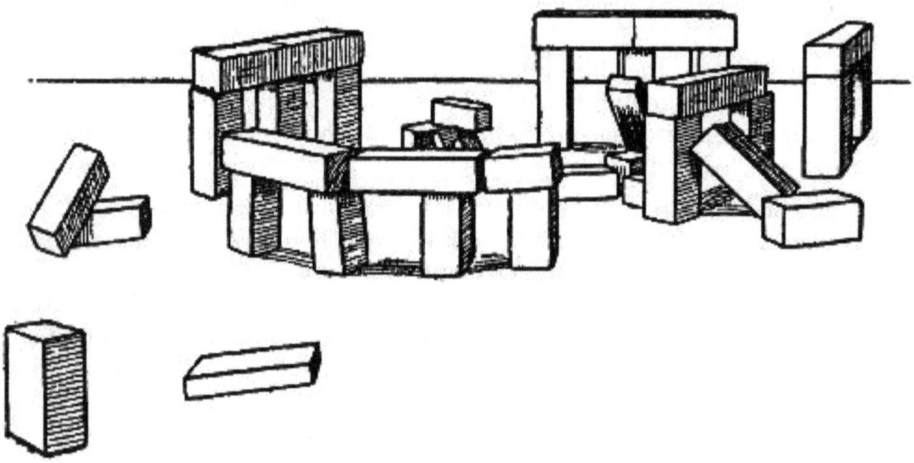

Stonehenge.

You loved your bricks, I think, especially if you lived in the days when bricks were of well-seasoned oak, heavy, firm, exactly proportioned, before the boxes of inexact light deal bricks, with the one painted glass window, began to be made in Germany. How finely those great bricks stood for Stonehenge, and how submissively Anna, the Dutch doll, whose arms and legs were gone, played the part of the Sacrifice. If you remember those bricks you will remember the polished, white wooden dairy sets in oval white boxes—churns and tubs and kettles and pots all neatly and beautifully turned. You will remember the doll's house furniture, rosewood, duly mitred and dovetailed, fine cabinet-makers' work, little beautiful models of beautiful things. Now the dolls' house furniture is glued together. You can't trust a light-weight china doll to sit on the kitchen chairs.... But you can get your mechanical ostrich and your golliwog....

Children in towns are cut off, at least for most of the year, from the splendid and ever-varying possibilities of clay and mud and sand, oak-apples and snow-berries, acorn-cups and seaweed, shells and sticks and stones which serve and foster the creative instinct, the thousand adjuncts to that play which is dream and reality in one.

For them, even more than for the happier country children, it is good to choose toys which shall possess, above and before all, the one supreme quality of a good toy. Let it be a toy that is not merely itself, like the ostrich of whom I hope you are now as weary as I, but a toy that can be, at need, other things. A toy, in fine, that your child can, in the fullest and most satisfying sense, play with.

CHAPTER IV

IMAGINATION

To the child, from the beginning, life is the unfolding of one vast mystery; to him our stalest commonplaces are great news, our dullest facts prismatic wonders. To the baby who has never seen a red ball, a red ball is a marvel, new and magnificent as ever the golden apples were to Hercules.

You show the child many things, all strange, all entrancing; it sees, it hears, it touches; it learns to co-ordinate sight and touch and hearing. You tell it tales of the things it cannot see and hear and touch, of men "that it may never meet, of lands that it shall never see"; strange black and brown and yellow people whose dress is not the dress of mother or nurse—strange glowing yellow lands where the sun burns like fire, and flowers grow that are not like the flowers in the fields at home. You tell it that the stars, which look like pin-holes in the floor of heaven, are really great lonely worlds, millions of miles away; that the earth, which the child can see for itself to be flat, is really round; that nuts fall from the trees because of the force of gravitation, and not, as reason would suggest, merely because there is nothing to hold them up. And the child believes; it believes all the seeming miracles.

Then you tell it of other things no more miraculous and no less; of fairies, and dragons, and enchantments, of spells and magic, of flying carpets and invisible swords. The child believes in these wonders likewise. Why not? If very big men live in Patagonia, why should not very little men live in flower-bells? If electricity can move unseen through the air, why not carpets? The child's memory becomes a store-house of beautiful and wonderful things which are or have been in the visible universe, or in that greater universe, the mind of man. Life will teach the child, soon enough, to distinguish between the two.

But there are those who are not as you and I. These say that all the enchanting fairy romances are lies, that nothing is real that cannot be measured or weighed, seen or heard or handled. Such make their idols of stocks and stones, and are blind and deaf to the things of the spirit. These hard-fingered materialists crush the beautiful butterfly wings of imagination, insisting that pork and pews and public-houses are more real than poetry; that a looking-glass is more real than love, a viper than valour. These Gradgrinds give to the children the stones which they call facts, and deny to the little ones the daily bread of dreams.

Of the immeasurable value of imagination as a means to the development of the loveliest virtues, to the uprooting of the ugliest and meanest sins, there is here no space to speak. But the gain in sheer happiness is more quickly set forth. Imagination, duly fostered and trained, is to the world of visible wonder and beauty what the inner light is to the Japanese lantern. It transfigures everything into a glory that is only not magic to us because we know Who kindled the inner light, Who set up for us the splendid lantern of this world.

But Mr. Gradgrind prefers the lantern unlighted. Material facts are good enough for him. Until it comes to religion. And then, suddenly, the child who has been forbidden to believe in Jack the Giant Killer must believe in Goliath and David. There are no fairies, but you must believe that there are angels. The magic sword and the magic buckler are nonsense, but the child must not have any doubts about the breastplate of righteousness and the sword of the Spirit. What spiritual reaction do you expect when, after denying all the symbolic stories and legends, you suddenly confront your poor little Materialist with the Most Wonderful Story in the world?

The Tree like a Man.

If I had my way, children should be taught no facts unless they asked for them. Heaven knows they ask questions enough. They should just be taught the old wonder-stories, and learn their facts through these. Who wants to know about pumpkins until he has heard Cinderella? Why not tell the miracle of Jonah first, and let the child ask about the natural history of the whale afterwards, if he cares to hear it?

And one of the greatest helps to a small, inexperienced traveller in this sometimes dusty way is the likeness of things to each other. Your piece of thick bread and butter is a little stale, perhaps, and bores you; but, when you see that your first three bites have shaped it to the likeness of a bear or a beaver, dull teatime becomes interesting at once. A cloud that is like a face, a tree that is like an old man, a hill that is like an elephant's back, if you have things like these to look at, and look out for, how short the long walk becomes.

Poppy Doll.

And in the garden, when the columbine is a circle of doves, with spread wings and beaks that touch, when the foxglove flower is a little Puck's hat which will fit on your finger, when the snapdragon is not just a snapdragon, but a dragon that will snap, and the poppies can be made into dolls with black woolly hair and grass sashes—how the enchantment of the garden grows. The child will be all the more ready to hear about the seed vessels of the columbine when he has seen the doves, and the pollen of the poppy will have a double interest for her who has played with the woolly-haired dolls. Imagination gives to the child a world transfigured; let us leave it that radiant mystery for the little time that is granted.

Doves and Dragon.

I know a child whose parents are sad because she does not love arithmetic and history, but rather the beautiful dreams which the Gradgrinds call nonsense. Here are the verses I wrote for that child:

FOR DOLLY

WHO DOES NOT LEARN HER LESSONS

You see the fairies dancing in the fountain,
Laughing, leaping, sparkling with the spray.
You see the gnomes, at work beneath the mountain,
Make gold and silver and diamonds every day.
You see the angels, sliding down the moonbeams,
Bring white dreams, like sheaves of lilies fair.
You see the imps scarce seen against the noonbeams,
Rise from the bonfire's blue and liquid air.

All the enchantment, all the magic there is
Hid in trees and blossoms, to you is plain and true.
Dewdrops in lupin leaves are jewels for the fairies;
Every flower that blows is a miracle for you.
Air, earth, water, fire, spread their splendid wares for you.
Millions of magics beseech your little looks;
Every soul your winged soul meets, loves you and cares for you.
Ah! why must we clip those wings and dim those eyes with books?

Soon, soon enough, the magic lights grow dimmer,
Marsh mists arise to veil the radiant sky.
Dust of hard highways will veil the starry glimmer;
Tired hands will lay the folded magic by.
Storm winds will blow through those enchanted closes,

Fairies be crushed where weed and briar grow strong....
Leave her her crown of magic stars and roses,
Leave her her kingdom—she will not keep it long!

The Astrologer's Tower.

CHAPTER V

OF TAKING ROOT

WHEN the history of our time comes to be written, it may be that the historian, remarking our many faults and weaknesses, and seeking to find a reason for them, speculating on our civilisation as we now speculate on the civilisations of Rome and Egypt, will come to see that the poor blossoms of civic virtue which we put forth owe their meagreness and deformity to the fact that our lives are no longer permitted to take root in material possessions. Material possessions indeed we have—too much of them and too many of them—but they are rather a dust that overlays the leaves of life than a soil in which the roots of life can grow.

A certain solidness of character, a certain quiet force and confidence grow up naturally in the man who lives all his life in one house, grows all the flowers of his life in one garden. To plant a tree and know that if you live and tend it, you will gather fruit from it; that if you set out a thorn-hedge, it will be a fine thing when your little son has grown to be a man—these are pleasures which none but the very rich can now know. (And the rich who might enjoy these pleasures prefer to run about the country in motor cars.) That is why, for ordinary people, the word "neighbour" is ceasing to have any meaning. The man who occupies the villa partially detached from your own is not your neighbour. He only moved in a month or so ago, and you yourself will probably not be there next year. A house now is a thing to live in, not to love; and a neighbour a person to criticise, but not to befriend.

When people's lives were rooted in their houses and their gardens they were also rooted in their other possessions. And these possessions were thoughtfully chosen and carefully tended. You bought furniture to live with, and for your children to live with after you. You became familiar with it—it was adorned with memories, brightened with hopes; it, like your house and your garden, assumed then a warm friendliness of intimate individuality. In those days if you wanted to be smart, you bought a new carpet and curtains: now you "refurnish the drawing-room." If you have to move house, as you often do, it seems cheaper to sell most of your furniture and buy other, than it is to remove it, especially if the moving is caused by a rise of fortune.

The Silver Towers.

Furniture to Live With.

I do not attempt to explain it, but there is a certain quality in men who have taken root, who have lived with the same furniture, the same house, the same friends for many years, which you shall look for in vain in men who have travelled the world over and met hundreds of acquaintances. For you do not know a man by meeting him at an hotel, any more than you know a house by calling at it, or know a garden by walking along its paths. The knowledge of human nature of the man who has taken root may be narrow, but it will be deep. The unrooted man who lives in hotels and changes his familiars with his houses, will have a shallow familiarity with the veneer of acquaintances; he will not have learned to weigh and balance the inner worth of a friend.

In the same way I take it that a constant succession of new clothes is irritating and unsettling, especially to women. It fritters away the attention and exacerbates their natural frivolity. In other days when clothes were expensive, women bought few clothes, but those clothes were meant to last, and they did last. A silk dress often outlived the natural life of its first wearer. The knowledge that the question of dress will not be one to be almost weekly settled tends to calm the nerves and consolidate the character. Clothes are very cheap now—therefore women buy many new dresses, and throw the shoddy things away when, as they soon do, they grow shabby. Men are far more sensible. Every man knows the appeal of an old coat. So long as women are insensible to the appeal of an old gown, they need never hope to be considered, in stability of character, the equals of men.

The passion for ornaments—not ornament—is another of the unsettling factors in an unsettling age. The very existence of the "fancy shop" is not only a menace to, but an attack on the quiet dignity in the home. The hundreds of ugly, twisted, bizarre fancy articles which replace the old few serious "ornaments" are all so many tokens of the spirit of unrest which is born of, and in turn bears, our modern civilisation.

It is not, alas! presently possible for us as a nation to return to that calmer, more dignified state when the lives of men were rooted in their individual possessions, possessions adorned with memories of the past and cherished as legacies to the future. But I wish I could persuade women to buy good gowns and grow fond of them, to buy good chairs and tables, and to refrain from the orgy of the fancy shop. So much of life, of thought, of energy, of temper is taken up with the continual change of dress, house, furniture, ornaments, such a constant twittering of nerves goes on about all these things which do not matter. And the children, seeing their mother's gnat-like restlessness, themselves, in turn, seek change, not of ideas or of adjustments, but of possessions. Consider the acres of rubbish specially designed for children and spread out over the counters of countless toy-shops. Trivial, unsatisfying things, the fruit of a perverse and intense commercial ingenuity: things made to sell, and not to use.

When the child's birthday comes, relations send him presents—give him presents, and his nursery is littered with a fresh array of undesirable imbecilities—to make way for which the last harvest of the same empty husks is thrust aside in the bottom of the toy cupboard. And in a couple of days most of the flimsy stuff is broken, and the child is weary to death of it all. If he has any real toys, he will leave the glittering trash for nurse to put away and go back to those real toys.

When I was a child in the nursery we had—there were three of us—a large rocking horse, a large doll's house (with a wooden box as annexe), a Noah's Ark, dinner and tea things, a great chest of oak bricks, and a pestle and mortar. I cannot remember any other toys that pleased us. Dolls came and went, but they were not toys, they were characters, and now and then something of a clockwork nature strayed our way—to be broken up and disembowelled to meet the mechanical needs of the moment. I remember a desperate hour when I found that the walking doll from Paris had clockwork under her crinoline, and could not be comfortably taken to bed. I had a black-and-white china rabbit who was hard enough, in all conscience, but then he never pretended to be anything but a china rabbit, and I bought him with my own penny at Sandhurst Fair. He slept with me for seven or eight years, and when he was lost, with my play-box and the rest of its loved contents, on the journey from France to England, all the dignity of my thirteen years could not uphold me in that tragedy.

The Turquoise Temple.

It is a mistake to suppose that children are naturally fond of change. They love what they know. In strange places they suffer violently from home-sickness, even when their loved nurse or mother is with them. They want to get back to the house they know, the toys they know, the books they know. And the loves of children for their toys, especially the ones they take to bed with them, should be scrupulously respected. Children nowadays have insanitary, dusty Teddy Bears. I had a "rag doll," but she was stuffed with hair, and was washed once a fortnight, after which nurse put in her features again with a quill pen, and consoled me for any change in her expression by explaining that she was "growing up." My little son had a soap-stone mouse, and has it still.

The fewer toys a child has the more he will value them; and it is important that a child should value his toys if he is to begin to get out of them their *full* value. If his choice of objects be limited, he will use his imagination and ingenuity in making the objects available serve the purposes of such plays as he has in hand. Also it is well to remember that the supplementing of a child's own toys by other things, *lent for a time*, has considerable educational value. The child will learn quite easily that the difference between his and yours is not a difference between the attainable and the unattainable, but between the constant possession and the occasional possession. He will also learn to take care of the things which are lent to him, and, if he sees that you respect his possessions, will respect yours all the more in that some of them are, now and then, for a time and in a sense, his.

The generosity of aunts, uncles, and relations generally should be kindly but firmly turned into useful channels. The purchase of "fancy" things should be sternly discouraged.

With the rocking horse, the bricks, the doll's house, the cart or wheel-barrow, the tea and dinner set, the Noah's Ark and the puzzle maps, the nursery will be rudimentarily equipped. The supplementary equipment can be added as it is needed, not by the sporadic outbursts of unclish extravagance, but by well-considered and slow degrees, and by means in which the child participates. For we must never forget that the child loves, both in imagination and in fact, to create. All his dreams, his innocent pretendings and make-believes, will help his nature to unfold, and his hands in their clumsy efforts will help the dreams, which in turn will help the little hands.

CHAPTER VI

BEAUTY AND KNOWLEDGE

CLEVER young people find it amusing to sneer at the old-fashioned ideal of combining instruction with amusement—a stupid Victorian ideal, we are told, which a progressive generation has cast aside. Too hastily, perhaps—too inconsiderately. "Work while you work and play while you play" is a motto dealing with a big question, and one to which there are at least two sides. Entirely to divorce amusement and instruction—may not this tend to make the one dull and the other silly? In this, as in some other matters, our generation might well learn a little from its ancestors. In many ways no doubt we have far surpassed the simple ideals of our forefathers, but in the matter of amusements, in the matter of beauty, in the matter of teaching children things without boring them, or giving powders really and truly concealed in jam—have we advanced so much?

To begin with, the world is much uglier than it was. At least England is, and France, and Belgium, and Italy, and I do not suppose that Germany, so far ahead of us with airships, is far behind in the ugliness which seems to be, with the airship, the hall-mark of a really advanced nation.

We are proud, and justly, of the enormous advances made in the last sixty years in education, sanitation, and all the complicated and heavy machinery of the other 'ations, the 'ologies, and the 'isms; but in these other matters how is it with us? We have grown uglier, and the things which amuse no longer teach.

For a good many years now—more than three hundred—old men have said "Such things and such were better in our time." And always the young have disbelieved the saying, which in due course came from their own lips. Has it ever occurred to any one that the reason why old people say this is quite the simplest of all reasons? They say it because it is *true*, and true in our land in quite a special manner. The chariot wheels of advancing civilisation must always furrow some green fields, grind some fair flowers in the dust. But the chariot wheels in which civilisation to-day advances grows less and less like a chariot and more and more like a steam-roller, and unless we steer better there will very soon be few flowers left to us.

Those of us who have reached middle age already see that the old men spoke truly. Things are not what they were. Without dealing with frauds and adulterations and shoddy of all sorts we can see that things are not so good as they were, nor yet so beautiful.

And I do not think that this means just that we are growing old, and that the fingers of Time have rubbed the bloom from the fruit of Life. Because those things which must be now as they used to be, trees, leaves, rivers, and the laughter of little children, flowers, the sea at those points where piers are impracticable, and mountains—the ones stony and steep enough to resist the jerry-builder and the funicular railway—still hold all, and more than all, their old magic and delight.

It seems that it is not only that the ugly and unmeaning things have grown, like a filthy fungus, over the sheer beauty of the world, but that the things that people mean to be beautiful are not beautiful, and the things they mean to be interesting lack interest.

And the disease is universal: it attacks new things as well as old. The cinematographs even, newest of the new, as things went in the old world; already the canker has eaten them up. In the first year of Picture Palaces we all crowded to see beautiful pictures of beautiful places: Niagara, the Zambesi Falls, the Grand Cañon. The comic pieces were perhaps French, but they were certainly funny. Also we saw the way the world lived, when it was the other side of the world: "Elephants a-piling teak," naked savages, or as near naked as don't matter, moving in ceremonial dance before the idols that were the gods of their deep dangerous faith. Dramas of love and death and pity and poverty. Quite often in the early days the cinematograph tale was of some workman driven by want to the theft of a loaf. It is true that the story generally ended in his conviction and the adoption of his charming baby girl by the wife of the *Juge d'Instruction*, but all the same people saw some one poor and sad and tempted, and were sorry and sad for his sake. Also we had tales of Indians with men that rode amain, and horses that one longed to bestride, such beauties they were, all fire and delicate strong temperament. War dramas too there were, where the hero left his sweetheart, and turned coward perhaps, redeeming himself with magnificent completeness in the splendid *débâcle* of a forlorn hope. That is all over. Already the sordid, heavy hand that smears commercial commonplace on all the bright facets of romance has obscured the vivid possibilities of the cinematograph. We have now for fun the elaborate hurting of one American person by another American person; for scenery, American flat-iron buildings; for romance the incredibly unimportant emotions of fleshy American actresses and actors. There are two girls, good and bad; two men, bad and good. In the end the good man gets the good girl, which is, of course, as it should be, or would be if we could believe in any moral quality in these fat-faced impersonators. You don't care a bit who wins, but none the less, the four of them mouth and mop and mow and make faces at you through five interminable acts, and when the good young man marries the good young woman in a parlour grossly furnished according to American ideals, you feel that both of them are well punished for their unpardonable existence. All real and delicate romance has, we observe, been wiped out by the cinematograph.

The Hall of Pearl and Red.

It has long been the fashion to sneer at the Crystal Palace, and indeed the poor dear has gone from bad to worse. There are exhibitions there all exactly like all other exhibitions: Switch-backs, *Montagnes Russes*, Silhouettes, Tumble-scumbles, Weary waves, Threepenny thrills (where you hustle against strangers and shriek at the impact). But once the Crystal Palace was otherwise. In the Victorian days we sneer at, when our fathers could not see that there was any quarrel between knowledge and beauty, both of whom they loved, they built the Crystal Palace as a Temple vowed to these twin Deities of their worship. Think what the Crystal Palace was then. Think what its authors intended it to be. Think what, for a little time, it was. A place of beauty, a place where beauty and knowledge went hand in hand. It is quite true that a Brobdingnagian Conservatory does not seem so beautiful to us as it did to the Prince Consort and Sir Joseph Paxton. It is true that even in the palmiest days of the Crystal Palace you barked your shins over iron girders—painted a light blue, my memory assures me—and that the boards of the flooring were so far apart that you could lose, down the cracks of them, not only your weekly sixpence or your birthday shilling, but even the sudden unexpected cartwheel (do they still call a crown that?) contributed by an uncle almost more than human. It is true that the gravel of the paths in the "grounds" tired your feet and tried your temper, and that the adventure ended in a clinging to bony fingers and admonitions from nurse "not to drag so." But on the other hand....

Think of the imagination, the feeling for romance that went to the furnishing of the old Crystal Palace. There was a lake in the grounds of Penge Park. How would our twentieth century *entrepreneurs* deal with a lake? We need not pause to invent an answer. We know it would be something new and nasty. How did these despised mid-Victorians deal with it? They set up, amid the rocks and reeds and trees of the island in that lake, life-sized images of the wonders of a dead world. On a great stone crouched a Pterodactyl, his vast wings spread for flight. A mammoth sloth embraced a tree, and I give you my word that when you came on him from behind, you, in your six years, could hardly believe that he was not real, that he would not presently leave the tree and turn his attention to your bloused and belted self. (Little boys wore caps with peaks then, and blouses with embroidered collars.) Convinced, at last, by the cold feel of his flank to your fat little hand, that he was but stone, you kept, none the less, a memory of him that would last your life, and make his name, when you met it in a book, as thrilling as the name of a friend in the list of birthday honours. There was an Ichthyosaurus too, and another chap whose name I forget, but he had a scalloped crest all down his back to the end of his tail. And the Dinosaurus ... he had a round hole in his antediluvian stomach: and, with a brother—his own turn to come next, as in honour bound—to give you a leg-up, you could explore the roomy interior of the Dinosaur with feelings hardly to be surpassed by those of bandits in a cave. It is almost impossible to over-estimate the Dinosaurus as an educational influence. On your way back to the Palace itself you passed Water Temples surrounded by pools where water-lilies grew. Afterwards, when you read of tanks and lotuses and India, you knew what to think.

There were Sphinxes—the correct plural was told you by aunts, and you rejected it on the terrace—and, within, more smooth water with marble at the edge and more lilies, and goldfish, palms, and ferns, and humming pervasive music from the organ. There were groves or shrubberies; you entered them a-tremble with a fearful joy. You knew that round the next corner or the next would be black and brown and yellow men; savages, with their huts and their wives and their weapons, their looking-glass-pools and their reed tunics, so near you that it was only a step across a little barrier and you could pretend that you also were a black, a brown, or a yellow person, and not a little English child in a tunic, belt, and peaked cap. You never took the step, but none the less those savages were your foes and your friends, and when you met them in your geography you thrilled to the encounter.

Further, there were Courts; I first met Venus, the armless wonder of Milo, and Hermes, embodied vision of Praxiteles, and the Discobolus, whom we all love, and who is exactly like Mr. Graham Wallas in youth, in the Grecian Court. In the Egyptian Court there were pictured pillars, and the very word Egypt is to me for their sake a Word of Power to this day. And the Spanish Court, the court of the Alhambra, the lovely mosaic, the gold and the blue and the red, the fountain, the marble, the strange unnatural beauty of the horseshoe arches....

I shall never see the Alhambra now, but it is because of the Spanish Court at the Crystal Palace that there will always be an empty ache in my thought, an ache of the heart, a longing that is not all pain, at its name, a feeling like a beautiful dwarf despair, in that I never shall see that blue and red and golden glory, and the mystery of its strange mis-shapen arches that open to the whole world of dreams.

Say of the Mid-Victorians what you will; they did at least know, when they set them, the seeds of Romance. Think of Euston Station: those glorious pillars, the magnificent dream of an Egyptian building to loom through the Egyptian darkness of London's fogs. And the architecture of Egypt was too expensive, and Euston remains, a magnificent memorial—the child of genius stunted by finance.

There was Madame Tussaud's too, a close link with the French Revolution: the waxen heads of kings and democrats, the very guillotine itself. And Madame Tussaud's daughter, with the breathing breast that seemed alive, and the little old woman in the black bonnet, Madame herself, who had seen the rise of Republics and the deaths of kings. These things, last time I trod those halls, were put in the shade, their place usurped by vulgar tableaux, explaining to the bored spectators what happens to a vulgar young man with a wife whose skirt is much too short in front and her hair very badly done, if he leaves his home for the society of sirens and cardsharpers. The tableaux were cheap and nasty, and taught one nothing that one could not learn from the *Police News*.

A Chinese Temple.

Once there were nightingales that sang in the gardens on Loampit Hill. Now it is all villas. Once the Hilly Fields were hilly fields where the children played, and there were primroses. Once the road from Eltham to Woolwich was a grassy lane with hedges and big trees in the hedges, and wild pinks and Bethlehem stars, and ragged robin and campion. Now the trees are cut down and there are no more flowers. It is asphalt all the way, and here and there seats divided by iron rods so that tired tramps should not sleep on them. And the green fields by Mottingham where the kingcups used to grow, and the willows by the little stream, they are eaten up by yellow caterpillars of streets all alike, all horrible; while in London old handsome houses are tenements, and children play on the dirty doorsteps of them with dead mice and mutton bones for toys. In the country women wear men's tweed caps instead of sunbonnets, and Hinde's curlers by day instead of curl papers (which if you were pretty, looked like wreaths of white roses) by night. And everything is getting uglier and uglier. And no one seems to care. And only the old people remember that things were not always ugly, remember how different things were—once.

Therefore I would plead with all those who have to do with children to resist and to denounce uglification wherever they may meet with it, and to remember that there is knowledge which goes hand in hand with beauty. To show a child beautiful things, and to answer as well all the questions he will ask about them, to charm and thrill his imagination with pictures and statues and models of the wonders of the world, to familiarise the child with beauty, so that he knows ugliness when he meets it, and hates it for the outrage it is to the beauty he has known and loved ever since he was very little—this is worth doing. If we would make beauty the dear rule of a man's life, and ugliness the hated exception, we should make beauty as familiar to the child as the air he breathes, and if we associate knowledge with beauty the child will love them both.

CHAPTER VII

OF BUILDING AND OTHER MATTERS

A MOMENT of rapturous anticipation lights life when the kind aunt or uncle has given the bricks, when the flat, sliding lid has been slipped back, and the smooth wooden cubes and oblongs have tumbled resoundingly on table or floor.

"I am going to build a palace," says the child. Or a tower or a church. And, the highest hopes inspiring him, he sets out on the new adventure. But he does not build a palace or a church, or even a railway station. What he builds is a factory, or a wall, or, in the case of the terra-cotta bricks, a portion of a French gentleman's country villa—the kind you see dozens of along the railway between Paris and Versailles. And however strong the child's desire that what he shall build shall be a palace or a church, that is, something beautiful and romantic, what he does build will always be the last thing he does, or ought to, admire. The fault is in the materials. They are lacking both in quality and quantity. No box of bricks that can at present be bought for money will build anything that can satisfy an imaginative child. An ordinary box of bricks—a really handsome one—measures, say, 12 by 8 by 2 in. If anything admirable is to be built from this amount of material the material ought to be presented in very small cubes, oblongs and arches—say 1 in. by ½ in. for the largest bricks, and going down to ¼ by ¼ by ¼ in. Given these proportions a really pretty though undistinguished building might result. But in the box of bricks 12 by 8 by 2 in. the smallest cube measures ¾ in. and the largest brick 9 by ¾ by ¾ in. These long slabs of surface cannot be broken and disguised in such small buildings as the only ones which the materials are enough to build. Hence, the deadly monotony of façade, broken only by the three or, in the case of the really handsome box, five arches, and suggesting nothing so much as a "works" or a workhouse.

In the bricks themselves there is not enough variety. The stone bricks, it is true, have broken out into a variety of ugly shapes and a blue colour with which you can, if you like, build a Mansard roof. But a Mansard roof in a coarse ugly blue tint, is no thing of beauty. Besides, it needs a solid substructure to support it, and if you make your building solid, every brick in your box will be used up, and all you will have to show for it will be a partially built wing of a peculiarly undesirable villa residence, replete with every modern inconvenience. Nor must it be supposed that the difficulty can be met by adding more and more boxes of bricks. Add them, by all means; and the result will be a larger and probably an uglier factory, or a completed, and therefore more completely hideous, villa. Unless you are a millionaire, and have a toy cupboard as big as a pantechnicon, you will never have enough bricks to build up the solid masses which rest the eye, and give solidity and dignity to architecture. Among such solid masses *steps* are not the least important. Every child knows that a really good flight of steps will take half the bricks in his box and leave insufficient material for the edifice to which the steps were intended to lead up. The tall broad smooth wall, its quiet surface disturbed only by one or two windows, a flight of steps and a doorway, is for ever out of reach of the child who has only bricks wherewith to build.

The Square Tower.

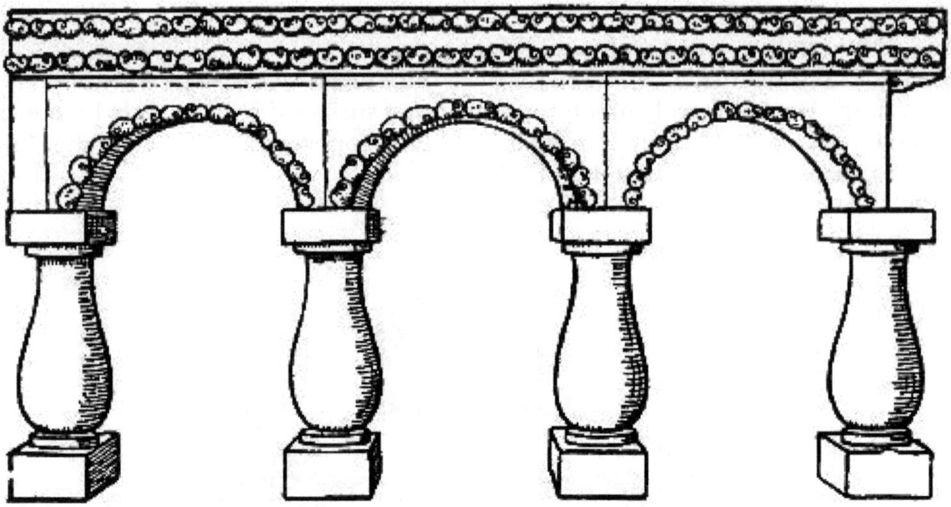

Shell Arches.

The arches supplied with boxes of bricks are usually few and badly proportioned. There is seldom any provision for setting them up in a colonnade.

The pillars which will support the ends of two arches are too wide for the *end* arch, which is single. This difficulty is dealt with in stone bricks, but not in wooden ones; at any rate so far as my experience goes.

There never was a time, one supposes, when so much money was spent on children and their toys. It is impossible to believe that, should some toy maker design and put on the market really desirable bricks for children, there would not be a ready sale for them. I suggest, then, that bricks are too large, and too small—and that what is needed is much smaller bricks, and much larger ones. The bricks in the old chest in our nursery started with 2-in. cubes, and went on in gradations of 2-in. to the largest brick—12 by 2 by 2 in. The chest itself must have been at least 4 by 2 by 1½ ft. Another detestable quality in our modern bricks is their inexactness—a sixteenth or even a quarter of an inch, more or less, is no more to the maker of bricks nowadays than it is to a bad dressmaker. Our bricks were well and truly cut: they were of seasoned oak, smooth and pleasant to touch—none of the rough-sawn edges which vex the hand and render the building unstable; they were heavy—a very important quality in bricks. They "stayed put." I suggest that such bricks as these, supplemented by arches of varied curves, but unvarying thicknesses, and slabs of board varying in breadth but not in length, would not be a toy beyond the purse of kind uncles and aunts, and certainly not beyond the means of our Council schools. The slabs of boards are to build steps with and to make roofs with. Every child who has ever built with bricks feels the reckless wastefulness of using for steps the bricks so much needed for walls and towers. And who has not experienced the aggravation of finding when his tower is built that he has used up all the long bricks near its foundation and has now none left which are long enough to lay across its summit and form its roof? The slabs of board should be, like the bricks, of seasoned oak, and should be an inch thick. There should be plenty of arches—so as to render possible some sort of resemblance to Norman and classical architecture.

But bricks alone, however beautiful and varied, cannot as building material have the value which material freely chosen would have. Children love to make mud pies, and to build sand castles, because the material is plastic and responds with more or less of docility to their demands upon it. Also there is always enough of it, which there never is of bricks, or for the matter of that, of plasticine. I can imagine a splendid happiness for a child in a bushel of plasticine—but the sticks of plasticine are too small to be made into anything architecturally satisfying; and much too expensive for ordinary children to have in any but such quantities as encourage niggling. You will notice that children never tire of building sand castles on the sea-shore—but they would soon tire of building with a quart of damp sand on a table. It is true that the sea washes away your sand castle, usually before it is finished, but its end is finely catastrophic and full of damp delightful incident. Also the climax has the great essential of drama—it is inevitable. How different the demolition of the brick-built house by mamma, who wants space for cutting out, or by Mary, who desires to lay the table. The most promising of palaces, the most beautiful of bridges, are, at the urgence of these grown-up needs, swept away, and so, never being able to finish anything, the builder becomes discouraged. Perhaps he takes to the floor as an eligible building site, only to find his buildings exposed to the tempestuous petticoat of Mary, or the carelessly stepping high-heeled shoes of mamma. The same thing happens with a dolls' school, or a dolls' dinner-party, or any game requiring pageantry of any sort—so that little girls who would like their dolls to be actors in some scene of magnificence find no safe place for the actors save in their arms—and nurse with enforced premature maternal fussings the doll who, in happier circumstances, might be a Druid or a martyr, or Francis the First at the Field of the Cloth of Gold. It is better to the child's mind that the cherished doll should safely be baby for ever, than that it should be Francis the First and get walked on.

In any house where space makes such a thing possible, a table might be set aside for children, to be their very own—a table on which neither food nor millinery should ever trespass. Of course it is needful that toys and pseudo-toys should be "put away" daily, but it is not necessary that they should all be put away. Those which are being used in some splendid half-developed scheme might surely be allowed to stay where they are, so that it may be possible to go on with the game next day. A truce might be called of that ruthless tidying up which, every day, destroys the new idea, and compels the child each day to produce a new scheme instead of allowing it to work on yesterday's and bring it to something a little nearer the perfection which it touched when the child's mind first conceived it. But, it may be urged, children leave everything half-finished, and go off to something else. Of course they do—but clear away the half-finished thing, and you will find when they come back from the butterfly flight after some other interest, that they will not be pleased with you.

"I've put all your bricks nicely away," you say proudly; and Tommy will say "Bother!" in his heart, even if his lips are sufficiently trained to avoid that expletive and to substitute: "I do wish you hadn't: I wanted to finish building my tower."

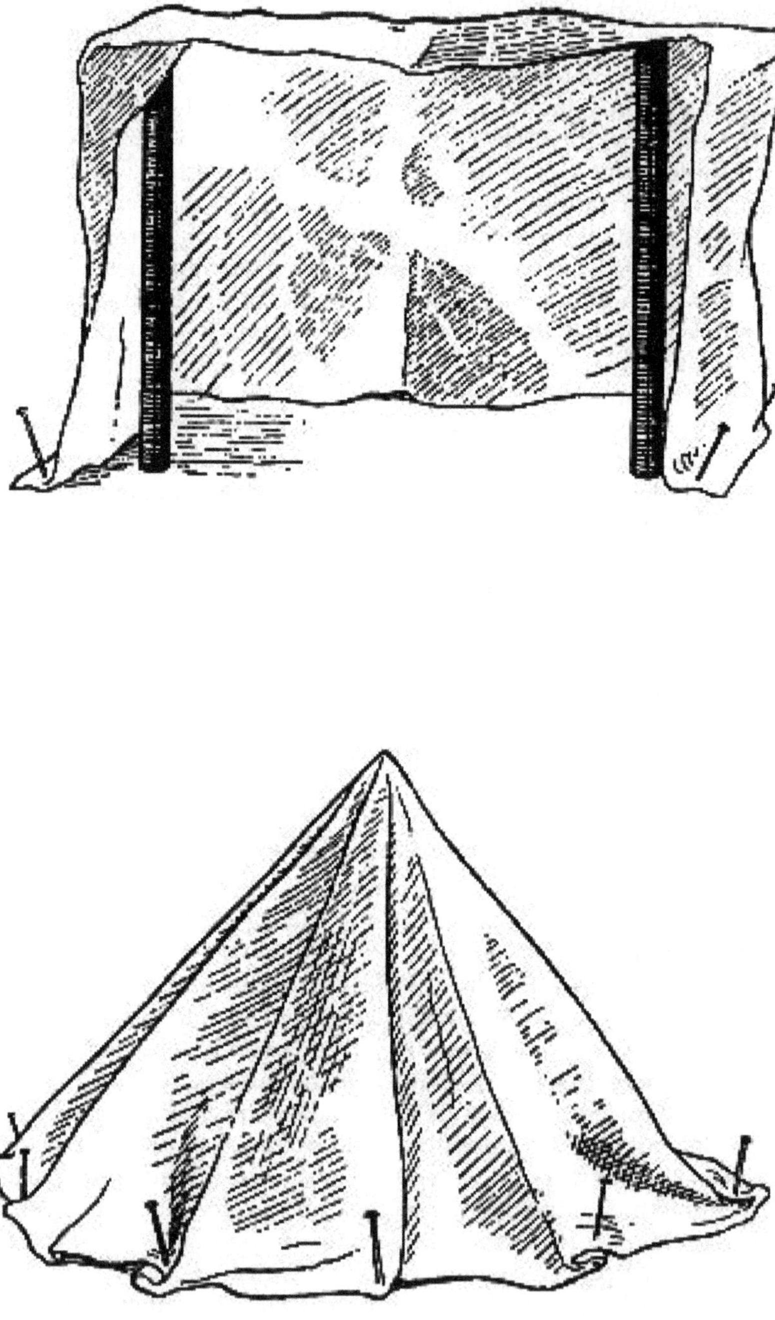

Handkerchief Tents.

You see one thing leads to another. It isn't that children are any more bird-witted than we are: it is that they have not yet learned to restrain the thousand curiosities, desires, and creative impulses proper to their age. You, of course, if you desired to set up a tableau of the Field of the Cloth of Gold, would sit down with a bit of pencil and the back of an envelope and jot down all the properties required for staging the scene. But the child who has "had" the Field "in History," and whose imagination has been stirred by the name of it—a thing that will happen under the stupidest of teachers—sets up Henry and Francis in paper crowns and only then begins to see that tents and banners and cloth of gold are lacking. Perhaps he goes off to the village shop to get flags, perhaps to your handkerchief case for tent-cloth, perhaps to the meadow beyond the orchard to gather buttercups. While on any of these quests some supremely important event may strike across his plans, and overshadow them—a new kitten, a gift from the gardener of plants for his little garden, or the fact that some one is going fishing. Then Francis and Henry are forgotten, the buttercups left dying on the doorstep, and the tent-cloth crammed into the pockets among string, stamps, acid drops, and pieces of the watch he took to pieces last holidays and never put together again, and he will follow the new trail. But he will come back to the Field of the Cloth of Gold, and if you have "tidied up" the kings and put their crowns in the wastepaper basket the child will be disappointed and worried, his imagination checked and his scheme baffled.

His annexation of your handkerchiefs will not occur if you have accustomed him to come to you or to his nurse for the means to his small ends; but if there is no one to whom he can apply for help, you will find that he will not stick at the sacred threshold of your handkerchief case. The tents of the Field of the Cloth of Gold will be far more important to him than the inviolability of that scented treasure-house—unless, of course, you happen to have explained to him exactly how much you dislike that your handkerchiefs should keep the sort of company they meet with in his pockets. Then, if he loves you, and has found you reasonable, he will refrain, while wondering at your prejudices. But he will—or ought to—find some other material for tents—letter paper perhaps. Letter paper makes quite good tents, though not nearly so good, of course, as handkerchiefs folded diagonally—supported by a central pole, say a penholder, and fastened down at the tucked-in corners with pins or rose thorns. You can explain to him that rose-thorns hurt handkerchiefs, but you will not punish him if this has not occurred to him. And this brings one to the question of crime and punishment, of which perhaps I had better say what I have to say before I go on talking about bricks and how to supplement them. As I was saying, one thing leads to another.

CHAPTER VIII

THE MORAL CODE

In attempting to explain and enforce a moral code, the first and most essential need is to formulate definitely to oneself the code which one proposes to enforce and to explain. There is nothing from which children, and subject human beings generally, suffer so much as the incoherence of the thought of those in authority over them. Before you can begin to lay down the law you must know what that law is, and your heart, soul, and spirit must not only know it, but approve it, before you can gain a willing obedience to it from those on whom you wish to impose it. By this I do not mean only that we ought to make up our minds whether this, that, or the other isolated act is right or wrong, as it occurs, but that we ought to have a clear perception and knowledge of the things that are right and the things that are wrong, and have a standard which we can apply to any new action brought under our notice, so that, measuring the new act by our old standard, we shall be able to say, with some sort of rough accuracy, "This is wrong," or "This is right."

And the standard of expediency is not a good one for this purpose, nor is the standard of custom, nor yet the standard of gentility or the standard of success in life. Children are not good judges of expediency. The law of mere custom will not be strong enough to bind them when desire calls with enchanting voice to forbidden things. Gentility and the gospel of getting on will leave them cold. You may at first deal merely with a succession of unrelated particulars, saying, "This is right," "This is wrong," beating down the children's questionings by your mere *Ipse dixit;* but a time will come when it will not be enough, in answer to their "Why is it wrong?" "Why is it right?" to answer "Because I say so." The child will want some other standard which he himself can apply. The standard of what you say may be a shifting one, and anyhow, he cannot be at all sure what you will say unless he knows what is your standard, the standard by which you will decide whether to say, in any given case, that a thing is wrong or right. And in order that you may clearly set before the child your own moral standard you must first have set it very clearly before yourself. It is not enough to say, "Stealing is wrong," "Lying is wrong," "Greediness is wrong." If you feel that these things are wrong because they are contrary to the will of God, you will not find that that explanation is sufficient for a child unless he knows very much more about God than His name and certain miraculous and incomprehensible attributes of His. He will want to know what is the will of God, to which these wrong things are contrary. And he will want very much to know the definite right as well as the definite wrong. You will have to give the child a standard that can be applied to positives as well as negatives.

There is a very simple standard by which to measure the actions of children—and, much more severely, our own actions. It is set up in the words of Christ: "Do unto others as you would they should do unto you"—a standard so simple that quite little children can understand and apply it, a standard so severe that were it understood and applied by us who are no longer children, the warped, tangled, rotten web we call civilisation could not endure for a day. There is no other standard by which a child can judge its own actions, and yours, and judge them justly.

Having fixed your standard it will be necessary to try your own actions by it as well as the child's. And this standard will give you the only vital code of morality, because it compels the continual exercise of imagination, the continual preening and flight of the wings of the soul. You cannot order your life by that Divine precept without a hundred times a day asking yourself, "How should *I* like that, if I were not myself?" without continually putting yourself, imaginatively, in some one else's place. And when the child asks, "Why is it wrong to steal?" you can lead him to see how little he would like to have his own possessions stolen. When he asks, "Why is it wrong to lie?" you may teach him to imagine his own bitterness if others should deceive him. It is, of course, much easier to say, "It is wrong because I say so," or even "because God says so"; but if you want to mark it right or wrong, to grave it deeply and ineffaceably on the tables of the heart and the soul, teach the child to see for himself *how* things are right and wrong—and to judge of them by that one Divine and unfailing rule.

Of course even when the child knows what is right he will not always do it, any more than you do: and one of the questions to be considered is how you shall deal with those lapses from moral rectitude of which he, no less than you, will often be guilty. Punishments, the old savage punishments, were revenge, and nothing but revenge, a desire to "pay out" the offender, to take an eye for an eye, a tooth for a tooth. More humane and reasonable legislators have sought to prove that punishment is curative—that the fear of punishment will deter people from doing wrong. A distinguished official of the Home Office gave it as his opinion only the other day that punishment, no matter how severe, will not act as a deterrent, if there is ever so slight a chance of the criminal's escaping it. What would deter would be the *certainty* of punishment, however slight. Now since you are not omniscient you cannot pretend to your child that if he does wrong you are certain to know and to punish him: if you are silly enough to pretend it, he will find you out immediately, and estimate your lie at its true blackness. You can, however, without any pretence, assure him that if he does wrong he himself will know it, that it will make him feel unclean and nasty, and miserable till he is able to wash himself in the waters of repentance and forgiveness. That if he acts meanly and dirtily he will feel dirty and mean, and if he acts bravely and cleanly he will feel clean and brave. And he will find that what you say is true. But not unless you shall have succeeded in convincing him that your standard is a true standard, and that the things which that standard shows to be wrong are wrong indeed. Here is the highest work of the imagination: to teach the child so to put himself in the place of the one he has wronged that the knowledge of that wrong shall be its own punishment.

One Half of the City.

No one desires, of course, that a child should be always feeling his own moral pulse: if he has learned that there is a right and a wrong way he will not be always bothering about which way he may be living—it will be only when something goes amiss that he will stop and consider. Just as one does not stop to think whether one is breathing properly, only when one chokes one knows that one isn't.

Punishment, however, should not be confused with the consequences of action, and while children are yet too small to understand all that God may be to them, it is possible to show them the *consequences* of their misdeeds, magnifying these beyond the consequences of the act to be reprobated and thus pointing the general moral. I mean that one may honourably apply, to the small wrong-doings of childhood, the *sort* of consequences—proportioned, of course, to the wrong-doing—which would result from such wrong-doing on a larger scale by a grown-up person. It will be exceedingly troublesome and painful for you, but perhaps its painfulness to you may be the measure of its value to the child. For instance, Tommy steals a penny, knowing that to steal pennies is wrong. He is very little, and a penny is very little, and your impulse, if not to slap him, might be to tell him that he is a very naughty boy and have done with it. It will go to your heart to bring home to him the consequences of theft, especially as you cannot do it at once; but if, next time you are about to send him to the shop for something, you say, "No: I can't send you because you might steal my pennies as you did the other day"—this will be hateful for you to do—but it will show him more plainly than anything else what happens to people who steal. They are not trusted. And the same with lies. Show him that those who tell lies are not believed.

But, remembering how it felt to be a child, have pity, and do not teach him these lessons when any one else is there. Let the humiliation of them be a secret between you two alone. Only when a wrong has been done which demands a restitution or an amend should the soul of the child, shamed with wrong-doing, be exposed to alien eyes.

When we sit in judgment on the aggressions and on the shortcomings of others the first need is neither justice nor mercy, but imagination with self-knowledge. The judge should be able to put himself in the place of the accused, to perceive, by sympathetic vision, the point of view of the one who stands before the judgment-seat. The judge is an adult human being, and therefore has some knowledge of the mental and moral processes of human beings. He should use this knowledge; and when it comes to a grown-up judging a child, it is no less necessary for the judge to place himself imaginatively in the place of the small offender. And this cannot be done by imagination and self-consideration alone. Memory is needed. Let me say it again: there is only one way of understanding children; they cannot be understood by imagination, by observation, nor even by love. They can only be understood by memory. Only by remembering how you felt and thought when you yourself were a child can you arrive at any understanding of the thoughts and feelings of children. When you were a child you suffered intensely from injustice, from want of understanding, in your grown-up censors. You were punished when you had not meant to do wrong: you escaped punishment when you had not meant to do right. The whole scheme of grown-up law seemed to you, and very likely was, arbitrary and incomprehensible. And you suffered from it desperately. So much that, even if you have now forgotten all that you suffered, the mark of that suffering none the less remains on your soul to this day.

It would seem that the humiliations, the mortifications endured in childhood leave an ineffaceable brand on the spirit. How then can we not remember, and, remembering, refrain from hurting other children as we were hurt?

The spirit of the child is sensitive to the slightest change in the atmosphere about him. You can convey disapproval quite easily—and approval also. But while most parents and guardians are constantly alive to the necessity for expressing disapproval and inflicting punishment, the other side of the medal seems to be hidden from them.

The most prevalent idea of training children is the idea of prohibition and punishment. "You are not to do it! You will? Then take that!" the blow or punishment following, expresses simply and exactly the whole theory of moral education held by the mass of modern mothers. The vast mistake, both in the education of children and government of nations, is the heavy stress laid on the negative virtues. Also the fact that punishment follows on the failure *not* to do certain things—whereas no commensurate reward is offered even for success in *not* doing, let alone for success in active and honourable well-doing. The reward of negative virtue is negative also, and consists simply in non-punishment. The rewards of active virtue are, in the world of men, money and praise. But there are deeds for which money cannot pay, and sometimes these are rewarded by medals and paragraphs in the newspapers—not at all the same thing as being rewarded by the praise of your fellow-men. Now children, like all sane human beings, love praise. They love it more keenly perhaps than other human beings because their natural craving for it has not been overlaid with false modesties and shames. They have not learned that

> Praise to the face
> Is open disgrace.

On the contrary, praise to the face seems to them natural, right, and altogether desirable. See that they get it.

Do you remember when you were little how you struggled to exercise some tiresome negative virtue, such as not biting your nails, not teasing the cat, not executing, with your school-boots, that heavy shuffling movement, so simply relieving to you, so mysteriously annoying to the grown-ups? Can you have forgotten how for ages and ages—three or four days, even—you refrained from drinking water with your mouth full of food, from leaving your handkerchief about in obvious spots natural and convenient, how you sternly denied yourself the pleasure of drawing your hoop stick along the front railings—because, though you enjoyed this musical exercise, others did not? And how, all through the interminable period of self-denial, you heartened yourself to these dismal refrainings by the warm comfortable thought, "*Won't* they be pleased?"—and how they never were. They took it all as a matter of course. To them, because they had forgotten how it felt to be a child, all your heroic sacrifices and renunciations counted as nothing. To them it was natural that a child should keep his fingers out of his mouth, and off the tail of Puss, should keep his feet still and his handkerchief in his pocket, should do the suitable things with meat, drink, and hoop-sticks. They never noticed, and so they never praised. But when, worn out by long abstinence from natural joys, natural relaxations, you broke one of those rules which seemed to you so useless and so arbitrary, then they noticed fast enough.

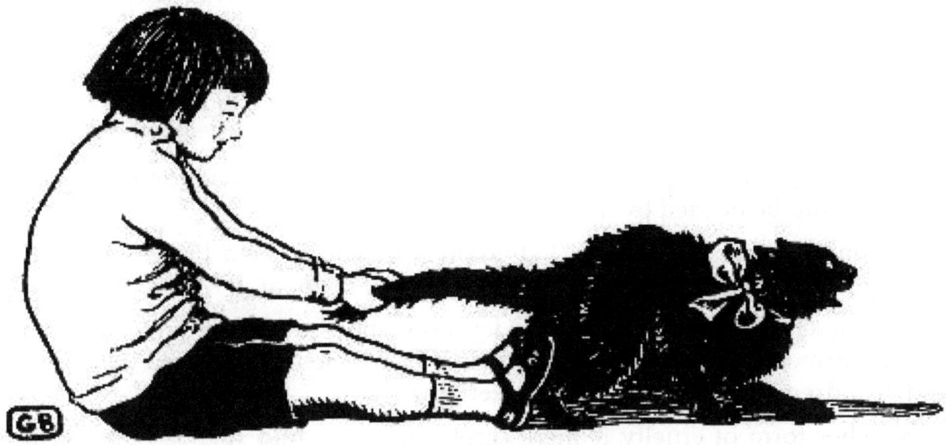

The Tail of Puss.

"Can you *never* remember," they said, "just a simple thing like not biting your nails?" Bitter aloes following, no doubt. Or, "I really should have thought," they would say, "that considering the number of times I've spoken about it you would remember not to make that frightful noise," with boots or hoop sticks or a blade of wet grass or what not. They did not pause to think, in their earnest grown-up business of "bringing the boy up," how many, how very many, and how seemingly silly, were the "don'ts" which you had to remember. But you will not be like that: you will notice and approve, and most needful of all, reward with praise the earnest, difficult refrainings of the child who is trying to please you: who is trying to learn the long table of your commandments all beginning with "Thou shalt not," and to practise them, not because these commandments appeal to him as reasonable or just or useful, but just because he loves you, wants to please you, and, deepest need of love, wants you to be pleased with him.

A hasty yet determined effort at putting yourself in his place is the thing needed every time you have to sit in judgment on the actions of another human being—most of all when that human being is a little child. If we cultivated this habit we should not hurt other people as we do. I have seen cruel things.

A little girl, suffering from a slight affection of the eye, was given by a sympathetic aunt the run of a box of that aunt's old ball-dresses. She spent a whole hour in arranging a costume which seemed to her to be of royal beauty. A crushed pink tulle dress, a many-coloured striped Roman sash, white satin slippers, put on over the black strapped shoes, and turning up very much at the toes. White gloves, very dirty and wrinkled like a tortoise's legs over the plump dimpled arms. Hair dressed high on the head over a pad of folded stockings, secured by hairpins borrowed from the housemaid. A wreath, of crushed red calico roses from somebody's last summer's hat, some pearl beads, the property of cook, and a blue heart out of a cracker—saved since Christmas.

"I am a beautiful Princess," said the child, and the housemaid responded heartily: "That you are, ducky, and no mistake. Go and show mother."

But mother, when she was told that this stumbling, long-tailed bundle of crushed finery was a beautiful Princess, laughed and said, "Princess Rag-Bag, I should say."

"It's only pretending, you know," the child explained, wondering why explanations should be needed by mother and not by Eliza.

The mother laughed again. "I shouldn't pretend to be a Princess with that great stye in my eye," she said, and thought no more about it.

But the child remembers to this day how she slunk away and tore off the beautiful Princess-clothes, and cried and cried and cried, and wished that she was dead. Children really do wish that, sometimes.

Another form of cruelty is mere carelessness. A child spends hours in preparing some surprise for you—decorates your room with flowers, not in the best taste perhaps, and fading maybe before your impatiently awaited arrival—or ties scarves and handkerchiefs to the banisters to represent flags at your home-coming.

"Very pretty, dear," you say carelessly, hardly looking—and the child sees that you hardly look, "and now clear it all away, there's a dear!"

The child clears it all away, and with the dying flowers something else is cleared away, something that will no more live again than will the faded flowers.

Be generous of praise—it is the dew that waters the budding flowers of kindness and love and unselfishness: it is to all that is best in the child the true Elixir of Life.

CHAPTER IX

PRAISE AND PUNISHMENT

While admitting that no pains can be too great, no labours too arduous to spend upon the education of the child, we must not shut our eyes to the fact that the sacrifice of the grown-up may often be better for him—or much more often her—than it is for the child for whom that sacrifice is made. There is a certain danger that the enthusiastic educator, passionately desiring to sacrifice her whole life, may incidentally, and quite without meaning it, sacrifice something very vital in the child. For the child whose every want is anticipated, whose every thought is considered, who is surrounded by the softness of love and the sweetness of sympathy, is not unlikely to disappoint and dismay the fond parent or guardian, pastor or master, by growing up selfish, cowardly, heartless and ungrateful; with no capacity for obedience, no power of endurance, no hardihood, no resource—whining in adversity and intolerable in success. The object of education is to fit the child for the life of the man. Once it was held that a rigorous discipline, enforced by violence, was the best preparation for the life which is never too easy or too soft. Now we have changed all that, and there is some danger that the pendulum may swing too far, and that the aim of education may come to mean only the ensuring of a happy childhood, without arming the child for the battle of life. It is right that to the educator the child should be the prime object, the centre of the universe, the prime consideration to which every other consideration must give way. But there is the danger that the child may become his own prime object, not only the centre of his own universe, but its circumference, and cherish, deeply rooted in his inmost soul, the conviction that all other considerations should and will give way to his desires.

Life, we know, will teach him, in her rough, hard school, that he is only the centre of his own universe in that sense in which the same is true of us all—that far from being the prime object of the world which surrounds him, he himself counts for little or nothing, except to those who love him—and that the consideration he receives will not be, as was the consideration lavished on him in his childhood, free, ungrudging, and invariable, but will be conditioned by the services he renders to others and the extent to which he can be to them pleasant or useful. Life, it is true, will teach him all this, but if her teaching be a course of lessons in a wholly new subject, they will be very difficult to learn, and the learning will hurt. Whereas if, from the very beginning, the child is taught to understand the interdependence of human beings, the fact that rights involve duties and that duties confer rights, he will be able to apply and to use for his own help the lessons which later life will teach him. More, he will have at the outset of life the advantage which one with a clear conception of rights and duties has over one who only sees life as a muddle and maze of things that are "jolly hard lines." They suffer as without hope who see that the world needs mending, and have never made up their minds what sort of world they would like. Whereas the child to whom, quite early, the lesson of human solidarity has been taught will, when he shall be a man, know very well what he wants, and will be able, however humbly, to help, in his day and generation, to re-mould the world to the fashion of his desire.

It is not difficult to teach children the duties of kindness and helpfulness to others, and the duty of public spirit and loyalty to their fellow-men. A healthy child is active, energetic, and deeply desirous of using his senses and his faculties. It is possible to assign to quite a small child certain duties, but the wise educator will manage to make such duties privileges and not tasks. The system of sentencing children to the performance of useful offices by way of punishment is abominable. It gives them for ever a distaste for that particular form of social service.

If we must punish, let us not permit the punishments to trench on the province of useful and, in good conditions, pleasant tasks. Give the boy an imposition rather than an order to weed the shrubbery walk; set the girl to learn a French verb rather than to hem dusters. The consciousness of being useful is very dear to children—it is worth while to feel and to show gratitude to them for all services rendered, and though it may be, as they say, more trouble than it is worth to teach the children to help effectually, that only means that it is more trouble than the help they give is worth. What is really valuable is the cultivation of the sense that it is a good and pleasant thing to help mother to wash up, to help father to water the geraniums, and, further, a thing which will make father and mother pleased and grateful. Children, like the rest of us, love to feel themselves important. Is it not well that they should feel themselves important as givers, and not as claimants only?

The tale of their public obligations may well begin with the lesson that it is part of the duty of a citizen to help to keep his city, his country, clean and beautiful. Therefore, we must not leave nasty traces of our presence in street or meadow—such traces as orange-peel, banana-skins, and the greasy bag that once held the bun or the bull's-eye. And it is quite as important to learn what we should as what we should not do. The idea and organisation of the Boy Scouts is a fine object-lesson in the way of training children to be good citizens. The duties of a citizen should be taught in all schools: they are more important than the latitude of Cathay and the industries of Kamskatka. Even the smallest children could learn something of this branch of education. I should like to write a little book of Moral Songs for Young Citizens, only I wouldn't call it that. The songs in it might take the place of "Mary had a little lamb" or whatever it is that they make the infants learn by heart. One of them might go something like this:

I must not steal, and I must learn
Nothing is mine that I do not earn.
I must try in work and play
To make things beautiful every day.
I must be kind to every one
And never let cruel things be done.
I must be brave, and I must try

> When I am hurt never to cry,
> And always laugh as much as I can
> And be glad that I'm going to be a man,
> To work for my living and help the rest,
> And never do less than my very best.

Another might begin:

> I must not litter the park or the street
> With bits of paper or things to eat:
> I must not pick the public flowers
> They are not *mine*, but they are *ours*. . . .

And so on. Simple rhymes learned when you are very young stay with you all your life. The duties and refrainings just touched on here might be elaborated in different poems. There might be one on being brave, and another on prompt obedience to the word of command. There is no position in life where the habit of obedience to your superior officer is not of value. To teach obedience without bullying would be quite easy: with very little children it could take the form of a game, in which a series of orders were given—for the performance of such actions as occur in the mulberry bush; and the competition among the children to be the first to obey the new order would quicken the child's mind and body, while the habit of obedience to the word of command would be firmly planted, so that it would grow with the child's growth and adapt itself to the needs of life. I would write more than one poem, I think, about the green country and the shame it is that those who should love and protect it desecrate it as they do. Let it be the pride of the child that he is not of the sort of people who leave greasy papers lying about in woods, broken bottles in meadows, and old sardine tins among the rushes at the margin of cool streams. Such people touch no foot of land that they do not desecrate and defile. Wherever they are suffered to be, there they leave behind them the vilest leavings. Filthy papers, the rinds and skins of fruit, crusts and parings, jagged tins, smashed bottles, straw and shavings and empty stained cardboard boxes. They leave it all, openly and shamelessly, making the magic meadows sordid as a suburb, and carrying into the very heart of the country the vulgarities of the street corner. It is time, indeed, that certain of the finer duties of citizenship were taught in all schools, Harrow as well as Houndsditch, Eton as well as Borstal. And one of the first of these is the keeping of the beauty of beautiful places unsmirched, the duty of preserving for others the beauty which we ourselves admire, the duty of burning bits of paper and burying pieces of orange-peel. If there is not time to teach geography as well as the duties and decencies of a citizen, the geography should go, and the duties and decencies be taught. For what is the use of knowing the names of places if you do not know that places should be beautiful, and what is the use of knowing how many counties there are in England unless you know also that every field and every tree and every stream in every one of those counties is a precious gift of God not to be desecrated by shameless refuse and garbage, but to be cared for as one cares for one's garden, and loved, as one should love every inch of our England, this garden-land more beautiful than any garden in the world?

The Other Half of the City.

A child should be taught to read almost as soon as it has learned to speak. I can remember my fourth birthday, but I cannot remember a time when I could not read. Without going into details as to the merits of different methods of teaching, I may say that a good many words may be taught before it is necessary to teach the letters—that reading should precede spelling—that CAT should be presented whole, as the symbol of Cat—and that the dissection of it into C.A.T. should come later. I believe that children taught in this way, and taught young, will not in after life be tortured by the difficulties of spelling. They will spell naturally, as they speak or walk. Of the value of the accomplishment of reading, as a let-off to parents and guardians, it would be impossible to speak too highly. It keeps the child busy, amused, still and quiet. The value to the child himself is not less. Nor is it only that the matter of his reading stores his mind with new material. To him also it is a good thing that he should sometimes be still and quiet, and at the same time interested and occupied. Of books for little children there are plenty—not fine literature, it is true—but harmless. As the child grows older he will want more books, and different books—and if you insist on personally conducting him on his grand tour through literature he will probably miss a good many places that he would like to go to. For a child from ten onwards it is no bad thing to give the run of a good general library. When he has exhausted the story books he will read the ballads, the histories and the travels, and may even nibble at science, poetry, or philosophy. I myself, at the age of thirteen, browsed contentedly in such a library—where Percy's anecdotes in thirty-nine volumes or so divided my attention with Hume, Locke and Berkeley. I even read Burton's *Anatomy of Melancholy*, and was none the worse for it. It is astonishing how little harm comes to children through books. Unless they have been taught by servants' chatter how to look for the "harm," they do not find it. I do not mean that absolutely every book is fit for a child's reading, but if you allow the reading of the Old Testament it is mere imbecility to insist that all the rest of your child's reading shall ignore the facts of life. You can always have a locked book-case if you choose: only see to it that the doors are not of glass, for the forbidden is always the desired.

As regards the facts of life, by which I mean the physiological facts about which there is so much needless and vain concealment, there is, it seems to me, only one rule. If your child has learned to love and trust you it will come to you with its questions, instead of going to the housemaid or the groom. Answer all its questions truthfully, even at the cost of a little trouble in formulating your answers. Do not leave the child to learn the truth about its body and its birth from vulgar and tainted sources. There is absolutely nothing that you cannot decently tell a child when it has reached the age when it understands that certain things are not fit subjects for public conversation—and until it has reached that age it will not ask that sort of questions. There is no difficulty in making children understand that their digestive processes are not to be discussed in general society, and it is quite easy to explain to them that other physiological processes are also to be avoided as subjects for general conversation. The Cat and her family will help you to explain all that the child wants to know. The child should be taught that its body is the Temple of the Holy Ghost, and that it is our duty to keep our bodies healthy, clean, and well-exercised, just as we should try to keep our minds strong and active, and our hearts tender and pure. And one need not always "talk down" to children: they understand far better than you think. They are always flattered by talk that rises now and then above the level of their understanding. And if they do not understand they will tell you so, and you can simplify. In talking of the subjects which interest them, you need not be afraid of being too clever. For even if they do not ask, your instinct and the child's eyes will, if there be love and trust between you, tell you when you are getting out of its depth. But there must be love and trust: without that all education outside book-learning is for ever impossible.

CHAPTER X

THE ONE THING NEEDFUL

THE most ardent advocate of our present civilisation, the blindest worshipper of what we call progress, can hardly fail to be aware of the steadily increasing and brutal ugliness of life. Civilisation, whatever else it is, is a state in which a few people have the chance of living beautifully—those who take that chance are fewer still—and the enormous majority live, by no choice or will of their own, lives which at the best are uncomfortable, anxious, and lacking in beauty, and at the worst are so ugly, diseased, desperate, and wretched that those who feel their condition most can hardly bear to think of them, and those who have not imagination enough to feel it fully yet cannot bear it unless they succeed in persuading themselves that the poor of this world are the heirs of the next, while hoping, at the same time, that a portion of Lazarus's heavenly legacy may, after all, be reserved for Dives.

The hideous disfigurement of lovely hills and dales with factories and mines and pot banks—coal, cinder, and slag; the defilement of bright rivers with the refuse of oil and dye works; the eating up of the green country by greedy, long, creeping yellow caterpillars of streets; the smoke and fog that veil the sun in heaven; the sordid enamelled iron advertisements that scar the fields of earth—all the torn paper and straw and dirt and disorder spring from one root. And from the same root spring pride, anger, cruelty, and sycophancy, the mean subservience of the poor and the mean arrogance of the rich. As the fair face of the green country is disfigured by all this machinery which ministers to the hope of getting rich, so is the face of man marred by the fear of getting poor. Look at the faces you see in the street—old and young, gay and sad—on all there is the brand of anxiety, a terrible anxiety that never rests, a fear that never sleeps, the anxiety for the future: the fear of poverty for the rich, the fear of starvation for the poor. Think of the miles and miles of sordid squalor and suffering in the East of London—not in comfortable Whitechapel, but out Canning Town way; think of Barking and Plaistow and Plashet and Bow—then think of Park Lane and Bond Street. And if your eyes are not blinded, the West is no less terrible than the East. If you want to be sure of this, bring a hungry, ragged child from that Eastern land and set it outside a West End restaurant; let it press its dirty little face against the plate glass and gaze at the well-to-do people gorging and guzzling round the bright tables inside. The diners may be smart, the ragged child may be picturesque—but bring the two together, and consider the conjunction.

The Hideous Disfigurement.

And all this ugliness springs from the same cause. As Ruskin says: "We have forgotten God." We have therefore forgotten His attributes, mercy, loving-kindness, justice, truth, and beauty. Their names are still on our lips, but the great, stupid, crashing, blundering machine which we call civilisation knows them not. The Devil's gospel of *laissez-faire* still inspires the calloused heart of man. Each for himself, and Mammon for the foremost. We no longer care that life should be beautiful for all God's children—we wish it to be beautiful for us and forget who, as we wish that wish, becomes our foster-father. There can be no healing of the great wound in the body of mankind till each one of us would die rather than see the ugliness of a wound on the body of the least of these our brethren. But so dulled and stupefied is our sense of beauty, our sense of brotherhood, that our brother's wounds do not hurt us. We have not imagination enough to know how it feels to be wounded. Just as we have not imagination enough to see the green fields that lie crushed where Manchester sprawls in the smoke—the fair hills and streams on which has grown the loathsome fungus of Stockport.

Now I do believe that this insensitiveness to ugliness and misery, this blindness to wanton befouling of human life and the green world, comes less from the corruption of man's heart than from the emptiness of the teaching which man receives when he is good and little and a child. The teaching in our schools is almost wholly materialistic. The child is taught the botanical name of the orange—dissects it and its flower and perhaps learns the Latin names of the flower and fruit;

but it is not taught that oranges are things you will be pleased with yourself for giving up to some one who is thirstier than you are—or that to throw orange-peel on the pavement where some one may slip on it, fall and hurt himself, is as mean a trick as stealing a penny from a blind man. We teach the children about the wonders of gases and ethers, but we do not explain to them that furnaces ought to consume their own smoke, or why. The children learn of acids and starches, but not that it is a disgraceful thing to adulterate beer and bread. The rules of multiplication and subtraction are taught in schools, but not the old rule, "If any will not work, neither shall he eat."

Of Lovely Hills and Dales.

There is no dogmatical teaching. That means a diet of dry bones. It means that the child is never shown how to look for happiness in the performance of acts which do not, on the face of them, look as though they would make him happy. It is not explained to him that man's life and the will of God are like a poem—God writes a line and man must make the next line rhyme to it. When it does rhyme, then you get that happiness which can only come from harmony. And when you do your best to make your line rhyme and cannot—well, the Author of the first line knows that it was your best that you did. God is shown, when He is shown at all, to our modern children, as a sort of glorified head master, who will be tremendously down on you if you break the rules: alternatively as a sort of rich uncle who will give you things if you ask properly. He is not shown as the Father to whom you can tell everything.

If you are successful in your work you win a prize and go home to your people, and tell them that you are first in history, receiving their applause without shame.

If you are good at games or athletics you can tell your mates that you made two goals or eighty-three runs or whatever it is, and delight in their admiration. If you are an athlete the applause of the bystanders is your right and your reward.

But whom can you tell of the little intimate triumphs, the secret successes, the temptations resisted, the kind things done, the gentle refrainings, the noble darings of that struggling, bewildered, storm-tossed little thing you call your soul?

God, your Father, is the only person to whom you can talk of these. To him you can say: "Father, I wanted to pay Smith Minor out to-day for something he did last week, and I didn't because I thought You wouldn't like it. Are You pleased with Your boy?" Do they teach you this in schools or give you any hint or hope of what you will feel when your Father answers: "Yes, My son, I am pleased." Or do they teach you to say: "Father, I am sorry I was a beast to-day, and I'll try not to do it again"—and tell you that a Voice will answer, "I am sorry too, My son—but I am glad you told Me. Try again, dear lad. And let Me help you"?

As you show your Latin exes. to your master, so you should be taught to show the leaves of your life to the only One who can read and understand that blotted record. And if you learn to show that book every day there will be less and less in it that you mind showing, and more and more that will give you the glow and glory of the heart that comes to him who hears "Faithful and good, well done."

You cannot suppose that your life is rhyming with the will of God when you destroy the beauty of the country and of the lives of men so that you may get rich and you and your children may live without working.

Can you imagine a company promoter who should say: "Father, I have made a lot of money out of a company which has gone to pieces, and a lot of other people are ruined, but I know that there must always be rich and poor, and if I didn't do it some one else would"?

Or—"Father, I spoiled the green fields where children used to play and I have built a lot of streets of hideous and uncomfortable houses, but they are quite good enough for the working people. As long as they have such low wages they can't live like human beings. And Thou knowest, O Father, that wages are and must be regulated by the divine law of supply and demand."

Or—"Father, I have put sand in the sugar and poison in the beer, alum in the bread and water in the milk, all these being, as Thou knowest, Father, long-established trade customs."

Men can say these things to themselves and to each other, but there is One to whom they cannot say them. It is of Him and not only of the wonders of His Universe that I would have the children taught. But they are only taught of the wonders, not of the Wonder-worker.

It is not that there are none who could teach, no initiates of the great and simple mysteries, no keepers of the faith. There are such, but they are muzzled, and the detestable horrors of civilisation go on in a community which calls itself after the name of Christ. And so long as we have in our schools this materialistic teaching, so long shall we raise up generation after generation to support that civilisation and to keep it the damnable thing we know.

Talk goes on and goes on and goes on. There is talk now of a Great Measure for the Reform of National Education, much talk—there will be more. There will be much ink spilt, much breath wasted; we shall hear of Montessori and Froebel and Pestalozzi, of Science and the Classics, of opportunities of ladders of scholarships and prizes and endowments.

We shall hear how hard it is that the sons of the plumber should not be able to go to Oxford and how desirable it is that daughters of the dustman should sometimes take the Prix de Rome.

We shall be told how important are the telescope and the microscope, and how right it is that children should know all about their little insides. The one thing we shall not hear about will be the one thing needful.

A tottering Government may keep itself in power by such a measure, a defeated party may, by it, bring itself back to office, but such a measure will not keep the nation from perdition, nor bring back the soul of a man into the true way.

We may build up as we will schemes of Education and Instruction, add science to science, learning to learning, and facts to facts; but what we shall build will be only a dead body unless it be informed by the breath of the Spirit which maketh alive. For Education which teaches a man everything but how to live to the glory of God and the service of man is not Education, but only instruction; and it is the fruit of the tree, not of Life, but of Death.

PART II

CHAPTER I

ROMANCE IN GAMES

A SHARP distinction can be drawn between games with toys and games without them. In the latter the child's imagination has to supply everything, in the former it supplements or corrects the suggestion of the toy. But in both, as in every movement and desire of the natural child, it is imagination which tints the picture and makes the whole enterprise worth while.

In hide-and-seek, that oldest of games, and still more in its sister "I spy," a little live streak of fear brought down from who knows what wild ancestry lends to the game an excitement not to be found in games with bats and balls and nets and bails and straightforward trappings bought at shops. When you lurk in the shrubbery ready to spring out on the one who is hunting you, and to become in your turn the hunter, you are no longer a child, you are a red Indian or a Canadian settler, or a tiger or a black-fellow, according to the measure of your dreams and the nature of the latest book of your reading.

At this point it occurs to me that perhaps you who read may have forgotten the difference between "Hide-and-seek" and "I spy." Hide-and-seek is just what it says it is; half the players hide, and the others seek them and there's an end of it. It is an interesting game, but flat compared with "I spy." It has, however, this merit, that it can be played without those screams to which grown-ups are, usually, so averse. Whereas I defy any one to play "I spy" without screaming. Hide-and-seek is a calm game; the thing sought for might almost as well be an inanimate object: it is the game of stoats looking for pheasants' eggs, of bears looking for honey. But "I spy" is the game of enemy looking for enemy: it calls for the virtues of fortitude, endurance, courage—for the splendours of physical fitness, for aptness, for speed. In "I spy" half the players hide and the others seek; but they seek not an unresisting stationary object, but a keen, watchful retaliatory terror. They seek, in shrubbery and garden, behind summer-house and conservatory, in the shelter of tree, hedge, and arbour, for the enemy, and when that enemy is found the seeker does not just say, "Oh, here you are"—that ending the game. Far otherwise; the seeker in "I spy" goes warily, his heart in his mouth—for, the moment he sees a hider, he must shout "I spy," adding the hider's name. "I spy Jimmy!" he cries, and turning, flees at his best speed. The hidden one follows after—the hunted becoming in one swift terrible transition the hunter, and he who was the seeker flies with all the speed he may, across country, to the appointed "home." The quarry unearthed has become the pursuer and follows with yells. Grown-ups would always rather that you played hide-and-seek—and can you wonder? But sometimes they will concede to you "I spy" rights, and even join in the sport. It is always well, in playing any game where anything may be trampled, such as asparagus beds, or broken, such as windows, to have a grown-up or two on your side. And by "your," here, of course I mean children. The habit of years is not easily broken, and I am so much more used to writing *for* children than *of* them.

Chevy Chase is a good old-fashioned game of courage and adventure. Does any one play it now? No child can play it *con amore* who does not know who it was who

> When his legs were smitten off
> He fought upon his stumps,

and to what bold heart the bitterest drop in the cup of defeat was "Earl Percy sees my face— —"

All wreathed with romance are the song-games, "Nuts in May," "There came Three Knights," and the rest, where the up-and-down dancing movement and the song of marriage-by-capture ends in a hard jolly tug-of-war, and woe to the vanquished! This is a very old game—and there are many words to it. One set I know, but I never have known the end. Little boys in light trousers and short jackets and little girls in narrow frilled gowns used to play it on the village green a hundred years ago. This is how it began:

> Up and down the green grass
> This and that and thus,
> Come along, my pretty maid,
> And take a walk with us;
> You shall have a duck, my dear,
> And you shall have a drake,
> And you shall have a handsome man,
> For your father's sake.

My mother told me all of that song-game, and that is all of it that I can remember. She always said she would write it down, and I always thought there was plenty of time, and somehow there was not, and so I do not know the end. Perhaps Mr. Charles Marson, who first found out the Somerset folk-songs of which Mr. Somebody Else now so mysteriously gets all the credit, may know the end of these verses. If he does, and if he sees this, perhaps he will write and tell me.

This game of come and go and give and take is alive in France; witness the old song:

> Qu'est-ce qui passe ici si tard,
> Compagnons de la Marjolaine?
> Qu'est-ce qui passe ici si tard
> Toujours si gai?
>
> Ce sont les cavaliers du Roi,
> Compagnons de la Marjolaine.
> Ce sont les cavaliers du Roi
> Toujours si gais.

Et que veulent ces cavaliers,
Compagnons de la Marjolaine?
Et que veulent ces cavaliers
Toujours si gais?

Des jeunes filles à marier,
Compagnons de la Marjolaine;
Des jeunes filles à marier,
Toujours si gais.

And I have no doubt that stout Dutch children and German children with flaxen plaits, and small contadine, and Spanish and Swedish and Russian and Lithuanian babes all move rhythmically back and forth on their native greensward and rehearse the old story of the fair maid and the Knight "out to marry."

The Mulberry Bush is another of the old song-games, where play-acting is the soul of the adventure, and this too is everywhere. "A la claire fontaine," I remember as the French version, danced on wet days in the cloisters of the convent of my youth. Le Pont d'Avignon, a glorious game, with its impersonations of animals, has, as far as I know, no counterpart in this country.

All these games are active games: they can, of course, be played by sheer imitation, a sort of parrot-and-monkey aptitude will do it; but if they are to be enjoyed to the full, the imagination must have full play. To *be* a knight a-riding to fetch a fair lady is quite simple, and quite thrilling—just as to be a bear demands nothing but growls and a plantigrade activity in the performer to be a fearful joy to the non-bear.

Cricket and football, fives and racquets, the games that are played with things out of shops, do not need imagination to help them out. The games without bought accessories should perhaps rather be termed "plays" than games. And the more highly cultivated the imagination the more intensely joyous are the games. All sorts of acting, dressing-up, and pretending games depend entirely on the imagination, and it is well to encourage children to act scenes which they have observed, or heard about or read about. The smallest child will experience a real joy in putting its pinafore on wrong way round, call it a coat, and announce with pride that it is "Daddy going a tata."

In the dolls' tea-parties you will observe a careful copy or travesty of your own "company manners," and as the small minds are filled with tales of wonder and adventure, you will find them re-enacted, the nursery rocking chair serving as charger for the gallant knight, and nurse's hassock taking quite adequately the part of the dragon. A small sister can generally be relied on to be the captive princess, especially if handsome trappings go with the part—and a cobweb brush is an admirable spear. The princess will be released from her bonds in time to act as chief mourner at the funeral of the slain hassock, which can be carried down the river in a barge made of the nursery table wrong way up—with the nursery tablecloth for a sail—an admirable tableau certain to occur if any one has told the children the story of Elaine. That the dragon should have as sumptuous a funeral as Enoch Arden himself, need not surprise you: a funeral is a funeral, be the corpse canary, guinea pig, or hassock, and to a dead dragon are due all the honours we pay to a gallant if unfortunate antagonist. Not only fairy tales, but history will be acted. You will have Jane as Queen Eleanor sucking the poison from Jack's grubby paws, and Alice as an Arab physician curing the plague, represented by blobs of paint-water on the rigid arms of Robert. How beloved will be the grown-up who, passing by the scene, shall refrain from commenting on the deafening groans of the patient, and shall, instead, offer the physician a ribbon for his girdle or a plume from the dusting brush for his turban.

Exploring plays and all the plays which include wigwams and war paint are such as an intelligent grown-up will be able to intensify and add backbone to—for a child's fancy will naturally outrun his performance, and though he may imagine a feather head-dress or moccasins, he will be only too pleased that a grown-up should make the things for him with that strong, unerring touch to which his small experimenting hands cannot yet attain. All such games require numbers; your only lonely child cannot play Indians to the full. Two is better than one and more than two is better than two, up to the number of six or eight. People don't seem to see how important numbers are for play. They see it fast enough when it comes to schools, but a regular association of children for the purposes of play is not encouraged. In a large family of boys and girls it just happens happily, but an association of children from various homes generally means a predatory horde of boys: girls don't associate with unrelated girls in joyous play-adventures, and boys are apt to think that little girls who are not their sisters are either angels or muffs, and neither a muff nor an angel is what you want to play games with. Parents and guardians might do a great deal to render play-association possible: I suggest that house parties of children, where the utmost possible liberty should be given, would stimulate enormously the plays which encourage daring and initiative, and would teach boys that girls are not necessarily muffs or angels, and teach girls that boys are not all brutes.

Fathers and mothers sacrifice themselves every year in August; you see them doing it, heavily, definitely, with clenched teeth and a grim determination not to be selfish, and to spend a month with the children at the seaside, however much it may cost in time, temper, and money. The Browns go to Scarborough, their friends the Robinsons go to Wales, the Smiths are in Devonshire and the Joneses at Littlehampton. They all go to the same sort of lodgings, do the same sort of things, and lucky is the mother whose nerves are not worn very thin indeed before the holiday ends. Now suppose all these worthy and self-sacrificing parents agreed to pool their families and let Mr. and Mrs. Brown take charge of them all—in some jolly big house suited to the needs of so swollen a household. Sixteen children are really, in many ways, four times easier to manage than four—and at least forty times as easy to amuse. In fact, you don't need to amuse them—they will amuse themselves and each other: Mr. and Mrs. Brown will only have to adjust ebullitions.

Meanwhile the Smiths, Robinsons, and Joneses are having their holiday where they will. Their turn of having the children will come another year, when the Browns will be free to range the world in August, knowing that their children are safe and happy and are, thank you, having a much better time than they could have in small seaside lodgings, even with the undivided attention of their fathers and mothers. Besides, if I may for once take the part of the mothers instead of that of the children, what sort of holiday do you think the mother has, when to the ordinary routine of housekeeping at home are added the difficulties of housekeeping in unfamiliar surroundings, in a house of whose capabilities she has no experience, and with a landlady whose temper, as often as not, is as short as her tale of extras is long? The woman who works all the year round at the incredibly arduous task of making a home, answering week in and week out the constant, varying demands on all her complex mental and physical activities, does really deserve a real holiday. What is more, she needs it. She will be a better mother the rest of the year if she be allowed for that one month to be just a wife, and a wife on a holiday. The wife whose turn it is to take charge of the amalgamated families will find so great a change from the exclusive care of her own chickens that the change in itself will be a sort of holiday. And the children themselves, perhaps, will learn a little from the enforced separation from the fount of unselfish devotion, and appreciate their mother all the more if they have, be it only half-consciously, missed her a little even through the varied and joyous experiences of their month's house-party.

CHAPTER II

BUILDING CITIES

THE devotion of aunts has often stirred my admiration. The heroism of aunts deserves an epic. But this is, as you say, not the place to write that epic. Give me leave, however, to say that of all the heroic acts of the devoted aunt, none seems to me more magnificent than the self-sacrifice which nerves those delightful ladies to settle themselves down to play, in cold blood, with their nephews and nieces games bought at a shop, games in boxes. I am not talking of croquet, or even badminton, though these may be, and are, bought in boxes at shops. Nor do I wish to depreciate chess and draughts, nor even halma, the poor relation of draughts and chess, nor dominoes, which we all love. These games, so precious on wet days, or when other people have headaches, cannot be too highly prized, too assiduously cultivated.

The rigours of the seaside holiday, too often in wet weather a time of trial and temper, would be considerably mitigated if chess and chess-board, draughts, dominoes, and halma were packed in the trunks along with the serge suits, the sand-shoes, and the sun-bonnets. The games which I do so 'wonder and admire' to see aunts playing are the meaningless games with counters and dice: ill-balanced dice and roughly turned counters and boards that look like folding chequer-boards till you open them, and then you find all the ugliest colours divided into squares and circles or slabs, with snakes or motors or some other unpleasing devices on them. These games are all exactly the same in their primary qualities: the first of them that was invented had all the faults of all its successors. Yet dozens of new ones are invented every year, just to sell, and helpless children try to play them, knowing no better, and angel aunts abet them, knowing all.

Grown-ups suffer a great deal in playing with children: it is not the least charm of a magic city that a grown-up can play it and suffer nothing worse than the fatigue incidental to the bricklayer's calling. Of course, most grown-ups will say that they would rather be burnt at a slow fire, or play halma, than be bothered with magic cities. But that is only because they do not understand. Try the experiment the next time you are spending a wet week-end in a country house where there are children. Get the children to yourself and ask your hostess whether you may borrow what you want for a game. The library is the best place for building: there is almost certainly a large and steady table: also there are the books. I need not urge you to spare the elegantly bound volumes, and the prized first editions, and the priceless folios and duodecimos in their original calf and vellum. You will find plenty of books that nobody will mind your using—the old *Whitakers*, bound volumes of the *Cornhill* and *Temple Bar*—good solid blocks for the foundations of your city. If there be a pair of candlesticks or an inkstand which match, you may make a magnificent archway by setting up the candlesticks as pillars and laying the inkstand on the top. You can see how this is done in the picture of the Elephant Temple. Get the children to bring down the bricks and enlist a friendly parlour-maid to let you have the run of the china cupboard, or a footman, if you are in that sort of house, to bring you the things you want on a tray.

But it is much better if you can go alone over the house and choose what you really want. You invite the children to help you build, and to build themselves. If they have never built a magic city you will find that they will presently desert their plain brick edifices to watch the development of your palace or temple. They will offer suggestions, and quite soon they will offer objects. They will begin to look about the room with their sharp eyes—and about the house with their keen memory and imagination, and produce the sort of things that look like the sort of things they think you might like for your building. They will wander off, returning with needle-cases, little boxes, shells—and "Would this do for something?" is the word on every lip. They are soon as much absorbed in the building as you are—and I take it you are an enthusiast—and your magic city grows apace. Then after a little while a grown-up, bored and out of employment, will stray into the library with "Hullo! what are you kids up to with all this rubbish?" and stand with his hands in his pockets contemplating the building industry. If you answer him simply and kindly, and don't resent his choice of epithet, it is almost certain he will quite soon withdraw a hand from his pocket and reach out to touch your magic walls with "Wouldn't it be better like that?" Admit it, and in hardly any time at all you have him building on his own account. Another grown-up will stray in presently with the same question on his lips. He too will come to be bored and will remain to build, and by tea-time you will have collected every grown-up of the house-party—every grown-up, that is to say, with the right feeling for cities. It will surprise you to find how keen you will yourself become as the work goes on, and how it will call into play all your invention and your latent craftsmanship.

You will be amazed at the results you can achieve with quite dull-looking materials, and still more will you be surprised at the increasing interest and skill of the grown-ups. When it is time to dress for dinner you will feel a pang of positive despair at the thought that your beautiful city, the child of your dreams and skill, must be taken down. It is like the end of the magic of Cinderella when her coach became a pumpkin, her horses mice and her coachman a fat rat. Now your domes are once more mere basins, your fountain basins are ash-trays, your fountains are but silver pen-cases and their gleaming waters only strips of the tin-foil that comes off chocolate or cigarettes. The walls of your palaces go back into the book-cases, and their façades return to the dull obscurity of the brick-boxes. The doors and the animals who stood on guard at the door-ways and terraces, on plinths or pillars, share in the dark rattling seclusion where many a wooden tail has been broken, many a painted ear lost for ever, but the tidying up has to be done: unless your hostess is one of those rare and delightful people who see what their guests like and lets them do it. In that case she may say "Oh! what a pity to disturb the pretty thing! Why not let your city stay for a day or two, so that the children can build some more to it to-morrow. No, of course it won't be in the way—and wouldn't it be pretty if we lighted it up with fairy lights after dark?"

The Palace of Cats.

Guarded Arch.

Then your city really has a chance. The children will think of it till bed-time and fall asleep in the happy throes of their first town-planning.

You may think that I exaggerate the charms of magic cities, because I happened to invent them, and you may be afraid that my swan, if you ever make up your mind to adopt it, may turn out to be an ugly and dispiriting duckling. I assure you this is not so. I have never met a child who did not like building magic cities, and not many grown-ups. Of course the love of them grows, like other loves, and the longer you can keep the city standing, the fonder you and your playmates will get of it. It will grow more and more finished in detail, and the ugly make-shifts will be reorganised and made neat with an irreproachable neatness. If the magic city game were played in schools, as I think it ought to be, a long table—or series of tables—could easily be kept for it, and the city kept standing and be added to from day to day. But it will not be the same sort of city as the one you build in the house where the parlour-maid lives and still less the sort that happens in the house where there is a butler and many silver boxes and cups and candlesticks.

Now I come to write all this down it seems very trivial, and it will perhaps seem even more so when I come to tell you about the different things we made and used for magic cities. But it is not really trivial. I do not think I claim for the magic city game more than it justifies, and I will tell you, presently, why I think this. Of course, when you have finished your city, if you ever do finish it, you make up stories about it, and always, even when you are building it, you imagine how splendid it would be if you were small enough to walk through the arches of your city gates, to run along the little corridors of your city palaces. Of course, it would do quite as well if your city became big enough for you to run about in while still keeping your natural size—but it is somehow not really so cosy to think of.

When I had built my first three or four magic cities this idea of getting into the city—being, of course, correct citizen-size—lived with me so much that I wrote a story-book about it called *The Magic City*,[1] in which a boy and girl do really become the right size and enter into the city they have built. They have there all the adventures whose wraiths danced before me when I was building courts and making palm trees and finding out the many fine and fair uses of cowries and fir-cones.

This book, *The Magic City*, produced a curious effect. I hope I shall not look conceited (because really I am only proud) when I say that about my books I have had the dearest letters from children, saying pretty things about the stories in the prettiest way. It is one of the most heart-warming things in the world to get these letters and to answer them. And if I had letters like these I should have been only pleased and not disturbed. But the letters about the Magic City, though they were full of the pretty, awkward, delicious things that children write to the author of the books they like, held something else—a demand, severe and almost unanimous, to know how magic cities were built, and whether "children like us" could build one, and, if so, how? I got so many of these letters that I decided to build a magic city where any child, in London at any rate, could come and see it. And I built it at the Children's Welfare Exhibition which the *Daily News* arranged last year at Olympia. The history of that building would make a largish and intimate volume. The difficulties that beset a home-dweller when she goes out into the world, the anguish of misunderstandings which arise between the builder of magic cities and the people who lay linoleum and put up electric lights, the confusion which results from having packed in boxes and all mixed up the building materials which you are accustomed to look for as you need them in your own home, the extraordinary mass of people, the extraordinary kindness of people; for after all, it is the kindness which stands out. It is true that the gentleman who, very much isolated, fixed the electric lights, behaved exactly like an earthquake, upsetting two temples, a palace, and a tank with an educated seal in it. But then how more than a brother was the man who did the whitewash! It is true that the dictator with the linoleum—but I will not remember these things. Let me remember how many good friends I found among the keepers of the stalls, how a great personage of the *Daily News* came with his wife at the last despairing moment, and lent me the golden and ruby lamps from their dining-table, how the Boy Scouts "put themselves in four" to get me some cocoa-nuts for roofs of cottages, how their Scout Master gave me fourteen beautiful little ivory fishes with black eyes, to put in my silver paper ponds, how the basket-makers on the one side and the home hobbies on the other were to me as brothers, how the Cherry Blossom Boot Polish lady gave me hairpins and the

[1] Macmillans.

wardens of Messrs. W. H. Smith's bookstall gave me friendship, how the gifted boy-sculptor for the Plasticine stall, moved by sheer loving-kindness, rushed over one day and dumped a gorgeous prehistoric beast, modelled by his own hands, in the sands about my Siberian tomb, how the Queen of Portugal came and talked to me for half an hour in the most flattering French, while the Deity from the *Daily News* looked on benign.

These are things I can never forget. When the show opened I was feeling like a snail who has inadvertently come out without his shell. Think how all this kindness comforted and protected me. And then came the long stream of visitors—crowds of them—I don't know how many thousands, who came and looked at my magic city and asked questions, and looked and looked at it, looked and said things. It is because of what they said that I am writing about that show at all. They all liked the city except two, and I cannot think that those two were, in other respects, really nice people. And more than half of them asked whether I would not write a book about the magic city which I had built there, and which lay looking so real and romantic under the soft glow of the tinted lamps: not a story-book, but a book to tell other people how to make such cities. And I said I would tell all I knew in a book. And when I came to write I found that there were many other things that I wanted to write about children, and other things than magic cities, and I wrote them, and this is the book.

And the reason I am telling you all this is that my big magic city at Olympia showed me, more than anything else could have done, that the building of magic cities interests practically every one, young or old.

It is very difficult to say all this and yet not to feel that you will think that I am boasting about my magic city. But I want you to believe that it was very beautiful, and that you can build one just as beautiful or much more beautiful if you care to try it. It is such an easy game. Every one can play it. And every one likes it—even quite old people. By the way, I have been asked to build another city at Olympia in April, and I hope that it will be a prettier one even than the other which I loved so.

CHAPTER III

BRICKS—AND OTHER THINGS

It is a mistake when you are going to build a city to make too large a collection of building materials before you begin to build. If it is natural to you to express yourself by pencil lines on paper you might perhaps draw an outline of the masses of your city as you see them in the architect's vision or illumination which should precede all building, either of magic cities or municipal cab-shelters. Having roughly indicated on paper the general shape of your city as you look at it from the front—the shape it would have against the western sky at dusk (I think architects call this the elevation, don't they?)—you proceed to collect such material as will roughly indicate that shape on the table or other building-place. And here let me once more warn the builder new to his business not to be trapped by the splendid obvious bait of floor's wide space. To build palaces while prone on the stomach may be natural and easy to extreme youth. To grown-up people it is agonising and impossible. The floor has only two qualifications as a building site. It is large—larger at least than any of the pieces of furniture which stand on it—and it is flat. And when you have said that you have said all. Whereas the inconveniences of the floor as a place for building are innumerable. The floor is draughty, it is inaccessible, except from the attitude of the serpent, and the serpent's attitude, even if rich in a certain lax comfort, is most unfavourable for the steady use of both hands. If you want to see how unfavourable assume that attitude and try to build a card-house on the floor. You cannot do it. If you kneel—well, you know how hard the floor gets if you kneel on it for quite a little time; if you sit or squat your dress or your coat-tails insist on playing at earthquakes with your building. Also the city on the floor is liable to hostile invasion by cats or dogs or servants: to the crushing and scattering by short-sighted outsiders or people who rush into the room to look for something in a hurry. Think of a playful elephant in some Eastern court of carved pearl and ivory lattice; an elephant co-inciding with one of the more fanciful volcanic eruptions, and your conception will pale into placidity in the face of the spectacle of a normal puppy in a floor-built city. And on the floor things not only get broken, they get lost. Cotton reels roll under sofas, draughts bowl away into obscurity and are only found next day by the housemaid when she moves the fender, and not then, as often as not; chess kings are walked on and get their crowns chipped; card counters disappear for ever, and it is quite impossible for you to keep an eye on your materials when you are grovelling among them. Therefore build on a table—or tables. Tables of different shapes, heights, and sizes make beautiful sites for cities. And bureaux are good, if you may take the drawers out and empty the pigeon-holes. I remember a wonderful city we made once: it was called the "City of the Thousand Lights," and it was built on a bureau, two large tables and three other smaller ones, all connected by bridges in the handsomest way. (The lids of the brick boxes make excellent bridges and you can adorn them to your fancy, and make impressive gate-houses at each end.) The bureau was the Temple of Mung, and we sacrificed a pale pink animal from the Noah's Ark at the shrine of this, the most mysterious of the Gods of Pegana. The thousand lights—there were not a thousand, really, but there were many luminous towers, with windows of a still brighter glow. You make them by putting a night-light in a tumbler—a little water first by way of fire insurance—and surrounding the tumbler by a sheet of paper with windows and battlements and fixed to a cylindrical shape by pins. The paper cylinders are, of course, fitted on outside the tumblers so that there is no danger of fire. All the same it is better to let a grown-up do the luminous towers.

Having chosen your site and blocked out the mass of your buildings, you begin to collect the building material. For my own part I see the city I am going to build in the eye of the mind—or of the heart—so vividly and consistently that I never need to make notes of it on paper. I know when what I am building is not in accord with the vision, and then I pull it down. Truly in accord it never really is, but it approximates.

Now when you have seen the silhouette of your city and begin to look for stuff to build with, you will instantly find that everything you can lay your hands on is too small. The bricks, even the boxes which contained them, are suited for the detailed building which is to come later, but now you want something at once bigger and less conventionally proportioned. Now is the time to look for boxes—not the carved sandal-wood boxes in which aunts keep their pins, nor the smooth cedar-wood boxes in which uncles buy their cigars, though both these are excellent when you come to the details of your work, but for the mass you want real big boxes; if you have a large table, or tables, Tate's sugar boxes are not too large. Also there are the boxes in which starch is packed, and cocoa, and the flatter boxes which the lady at the sweet-shop will give you if she likes you, and sell to you for a penny anyhow. The boxes in which your father gets his collars, and the boxes in which your mother gets her chocolates, though not really large, should be collected at the same time, because they need the same treatment. I am assuming now that you are not building a city for an afternoon's amusement, but one for which you have found a safe resting place—a city that may take days to build and will not be disturbed for days. If you can once found your city in a safe place, and you are working at it day after day, you will go on thinking of more and more things to be added to it, and it will grow in beauty under your hands as naturally as a flower under the hand of summer.

You have now your collection of boxes—but they are of plain, rough wood, and probably disfigured by coarse coloured printed papers telling what the boxes once held. These papers you wash off, and when the boxes are clean and dry, you paint or colour-wash them to suit your requirements. Now your requirements are large blocks of colours to match your bricks, and bricks are of three colours—white, terra-cotta, and stone colour.

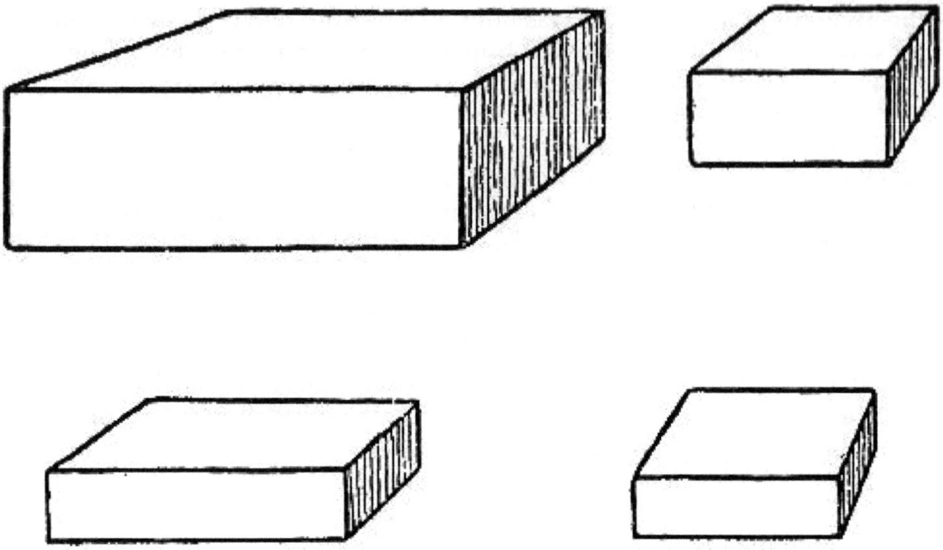

Boxes.

The stone bricks are stone colour and terra-cotta—oak bricks are very nearly stone colour—and there are white-wood bricks. To these three I would add a dark brown; and as this dark brown is not sold in boxes at the shops, you had better colour some of your bricks with it for yourself. Dark wood in a city gives a wonderful richness and helps the lighter colours more than you would think possible. A city in which some buildings are of dark wood will have an air of reality never achieved by a city where all is red or white or stone colour. By the way, among the stone bricks there are some blue ones, but you will always have enough of them, for they are the last things you will ever want to use.

Your boxes then must be coloured either white, red, stone colour, or dark brown. In the white use either white paint—flat, not shining, or if that cost too much trouble and money, whitewash made of whitening, size, hot water and a pinch of yellow ochre or chrome powder to give it a pleasant ivory creaminess. There should be a good deal of size so that the whitewash does not come off on every thing.

The red boxes can be painted to match the red bricks, or colour-washed (whitewash as before, but red ochre for colour).

Stone colour is not a very satisfactory tint and too much of it makes for gloom. The lids and bottoms of the brick boxes will generally give you as much of it as you want. But if you desire stone colour you can make it by putting a pinch of raw umber in the whitewash. Or you can paint your boxes with this uninteresting tint—resembling the doors of back kitchens. With these paints or colour-washes you can make your odd many-shaped boxes into smooth-surfaced blocks to match your bricks: and not only wooden, but cardboard boxes can be treated in this way. All these colours can be bought in gigantic penn'orths at the oil-shops. But when I come to the dark brown, which I confess is my favourite colour, no cardboard box will serve your turn. You must choose clean, smooth wood, because the brown colouring is transparent, and the grain will show through. Your bricks will be smooth enough, and if the boxes are not smooth a little sand-paper will soon subdue their rough exterior. I suppose you know how to use sand-paper? If you just rub with your fingers you hurt your fingers and don't make much progress; the best way is to wrap the sand-paper round a flat piece of wood—a wooden brick will do—and rub with that.

When your wood is all smooth you mix your stain. And here I make a present to all housewives of the best floor stain in the world. Get a tin of Brunswick black—the kind you put on stoves—and some turpentine. Mix a little of the black and a little of the turpentine in a pot and try it on the wood with a smooth brush—a flat brush is the best—till you have the colour you want, always remembering that it will be a little lighter when it is dry. When you have decided on the colour, paint your bricks and boxes on five out of their six sides lightly and smoothly, keeping to the grain of the wood, and not going over the same surface twice if you can help it. This is why a flat brush is the best: it will go right down the side of a brick and colour it at one sweep. Then stand each brick up on end to dry. When it is dry you can paint the under bit on which it has been standing. While you have stains and colours going it is well to colour some of your arches, and also such things as cotton-reels, and the little wooden pill-boxes that you get at the chemist's. Before colouring these boxes fill them with sand or stones and stick the lids on with glue. Otherwise they will not be heavy enough to build with happily.

This painting or colouring should be done out of doors, or in an out-house, if possible. If you have to do it in the house spread several thicknesses of newspaper before you begin, and make a calm resting place for your painted things where they can dry at leisure and not be scarred with the finger-marks of her who "clears away."

The earnest builder will keep a watchful eye on any carpentering that may go on in the house, and annex the smaller blocks of wood cut off the end of things, which, to an alien eye, are so much rubbish, but which are to the builder stores of price.

If there are a few shillings to spare, the carpenter will, for those few shillings, cut you certain shapes which you cannot buy in shops—arches of a comfortable thickness and of satisfying curves, and slabs of board for building steps. These should be of varying lengths and thicknesses and made in sets of twelve steps, with two boards to each step, twenty-four slabs to a set. The biggest might be 1 in. thick and the bottom and largest slabs 12 by 6 in., lessening to 6 by 1 in. The next set might be ¾ in., and of corresponding proportions, then ½ in., then ¼ in. The two basic slabs of the ¾ in. would be 9 by 4½ in., and those of the ½ in. would be 6 by 3 in. A set with ¼ in. steps (the basic slabs 3 by 1½ in.) would complete the set. Flights of steps of many varying heights and sizes could be built with these slabs. Ask the carpenter—if the shillings are forthcoming—to save for you the curved pieces of wood which come out of the arches. They are very useful for the bases of pillars, for towers and for the pedestals of statues or vases. Some of the arches, steps, and blocks should be coloured to match the red, white, and brown bricks.

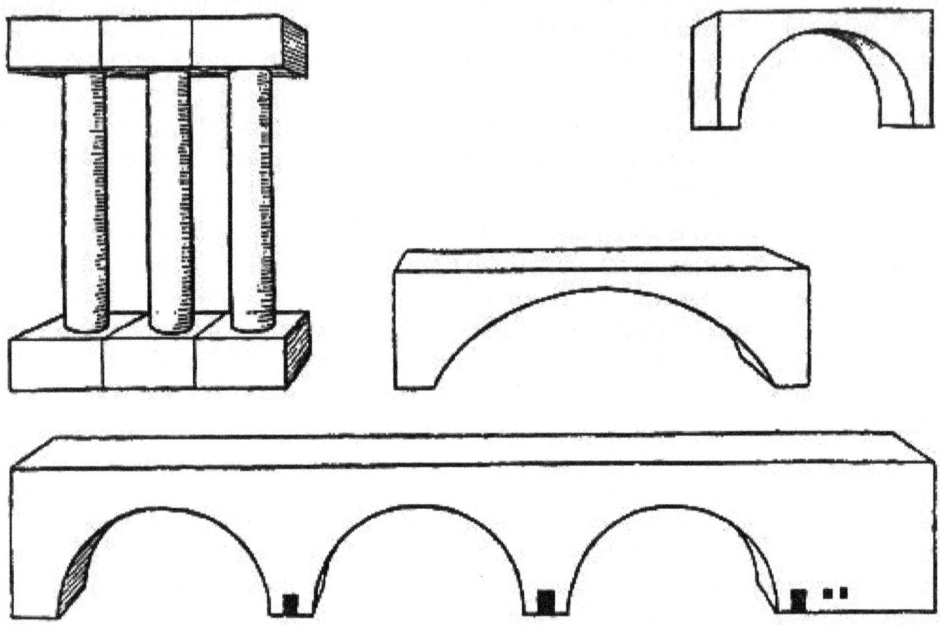

Arches and Pillars.

Some of the boxes, particularly the larger ones, should have doorways sawn in them on opposite sides—it is pleasant to look *through* a building and see the light beyond; and if you are a thorough builder you can make a pillared interior which will delight the eyes of those who stoop down and peer through the doorway. A few narrow, oblong windows, high up, will also be useful. You need not show them unless you wish: you can always conceal them by a façade of bricks.

Another pleasant use of a big box is to cut out the top and sides and make a columned court of it, which, when cream-washed, dignifies your city with almost all the glory that was Greece and the grandeur that was Rome. The columns are cut from broom-handles—twopence each at the oil-shop, or, in the case of smaller boxes, from those nice round smooth wooden sticks which cost a penny and are used in ordinary life to thread window-blinds on.

If you are going to make a city which is to stand for some time, a little thin glue is a good help to stability. If it is only a here-to-day-and-gone-to-morrow city, Plasticine is good—the least touch of it seeming to make things safe which otherwise might totter to their ruin. But except as mortar Plasticine should be shunned. It is not good as a building material.

Having now your bricks, boxes, arches, steps, and rounds, you may begin to block out your building. Quite soon you will begin to find that everything is too rectilinear. Even the arches and the rounds and the pillars and the pill-boxes cannot satisfy your desire for curves. This is the moment when you will begin to look about you for domes. And the domes, on the instant of their imposition in your building, will call out for minarets. It is then that you will wander about the house seeking eagerly for things that are like other things. Your search will be magnificently successful, if only the lady of the house has given you a free hand, and you have been so fortunate as to secure the sympathies of the kitchen queen.

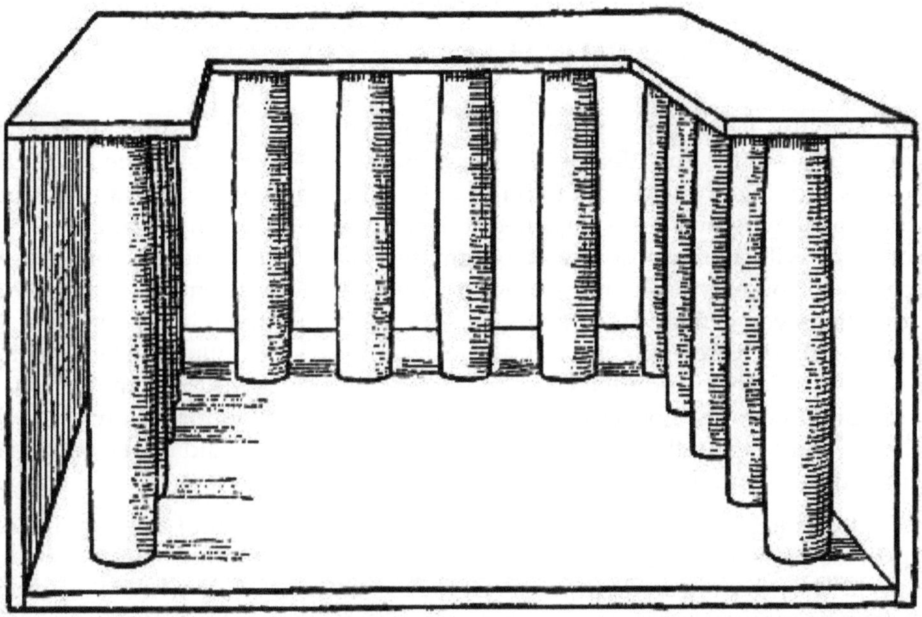

Pillared Court.

CHAPTER IV

THE MAGIC CITY

The only magic in the city is the magic of imagination, which is, after all, the best magic in the world. The idea of it came to me when I was dissatisfied with the materials provided for children to build with, and I think it must be a really true idea, because wherever I have applied it, it has worked, and that, I am told, is in accordance with the philosophy of pragmatism and a characteristic of all great discoveries. You may build magic cities in homes of modest comfort, using all the pretty things you can lay your hands on. You may build them in the mansions of the rich, if the rich are nice people and love cities, and if the butler will let you have the silver candlesticks for pillars, and the silver-gilt rose-bowls for domes; and you could build one in the houses of the very poor, if the very poor had any space for building—build them there and not use a single thing that could not be begged or borrowed by an intelligent child, no matter how poor.

Children love to build. I still think with fond affection, and I am afraid speak with tiresome repetition, of those big oak bricks which we had when we were children. They disappeared when we left the old London house where I was born. It was in Kennington, that house—and it had a big garden and a meadow and a cottage and a laundry, stables and cow-house and pig-styes, elm-trees and vines, tiger lilies and flags in the garden, and chrysanthemums that smelt like earth and hyacinths that smelt like heaven. Our nursery was at the top of the house, a big room with a pillar in the middle to support the roof. "The post," we called it: it was excellent for playing mulberry bush, or for being martyrs at. The skipping rope did to bind the martyrs to the stake. When we left that house we went to Brighton, where there was a small and gritty garden, where nothing grew but geraniums and calceolarias. And we did not have our bricks any more. Perhaps they were too heavy to move. Perhaps the Brighton house was too small for the chest. I think I must have clamoured for the old bricks, for I remember very well the advent of a small box of deal bricks made in Germany, which had indeed two arches and four pillars, and a square of glass framed in wood daubed with heavy, ugly body colour, and called a window. But you could not build with those bricks. So there was no building at Brighton except on the beach. Sand is as good as anything in the world to build with—but there is no sand on the beach at Brighton, only sandiness. There are stones—pebbles you call them, but they are too round to be piled up into buildings. The only thing you can play with them is dolls' dinner parties. There are plenty of oyster shells and flat bits of slate and tile for dishes and plates—and it is quite easy to find stones the proper shape and colour for boiled fowls and hams and roast legs of mutton, German sausages, ribs of beef, mince pies, pork pies, roast hare or calf's head. But building is impossible.

In the courtyard of our house in France there was an out-house with a sloping roof and a flat parapet about four feet high. We used to build little clay huts along this, and roof them with slates, leaving a hole for a chimney. The huts had holes for windows and doors, and we used to collect bits of candle and put them in our huts after dark and enjoy the lovely spectacle of our illuminated buildings till some one remembered us and caught us, and sent us to bed. That was the curse of our hut-building—the very splendour of the result attracted the attention one most wished to avoid. But clay was our only building material, and after the big bricks were lost I never had any more bricks till I had children of my own who had bricks of their own. And then I played with them and theirs. And even then I never thought of building magic cities till the Indian soldiers came.

They were very fine soldiers with turbans and swords and eyes that gleamed in quite a lifelike way, riding on horses of a violently active appearance: they came to my little son when he was getting well after measles or some such sorrow, and he wanted a fort built for them. So we rattled all the bricks out of their boxes on to the long cutting-out table in the work-room and began to build. But do what we would our fort would not look like a fort—at any rate not like an Eastern fort. We pulled it down and tried again, and then again, but no: regardless of our patient energy our fort quietly but persistently refused to look like anything but a factory—a building wholly unworthy of those military heroes with the prancing steeds and the coloured turbans, and the eyes with so much white in them. So then I wondered what was needed to give a hint of the gorgeous East to the fort, and I perceived that what was wanted was a dome—domes.

So I fetched some brass finger-bowls and lustre basins off the dresser in the dining-room and inverted one on the chief tower of our fort, and behold! the East began to sparkle and beckon. Domes called for minarets, and chessmen on pillars supplied the need. One thing led to another, and before the day was over the Indian horsemen were in full charge across a sanded plain where palm trees grew—a sanded plain bounded only by the edges of the table, along three sides of which were buildings that never rose beside the banks of Thames, but seemed quite suitable piles to reflect their fair proportions in the Ganges or the Sutlej, especially when viewed by eyes which had not had the privilege of gazing on those fair and distant streams.

I learned a great deal in that my first day of what I may term romantic building, but what I learned was the merest shadow-sketch of the possibilities of my discovery. My little son, for his part, learned that a bowl one way up is a bowl, a thing for a little boy to eat bread and milk out of; the other way up it is a dome for a king's palace. That books are not only things to read, but that they will make marble slabs for the building of temples. That chessmen are not only useful for playing that difficult and tedious game on which grown-ups are so slowly and silently intent, or even for playing all those other games, of soldiers, which will naturally occur to any one with command of the pleasant turned pieces. Chessmen, he learned, had other and less simple uses. As minarets of delicate carved work they lightened the mass of buildings and conferred elegance and distinction, converting what had been a block of bricks into a pavilion for a sultan or a tomb for a sultan's bride.

Materials for the Guard-Room.

There was a little guard-room, I remember, at the corner of our first city, and there has been a little guard-room at the corner of every city we have built since. In simple beauty, that little guard-room seemed to us then to touch perfection. And really, you know, I have not yet been able to improve on it. The material was simplicity itself: six books, five chessmen, and a basin; and you see here how the guard-room looked when it was done.

The Guard Room.

The Domino Door.

There was a black box, I remember, standing on another box, with domino steps. It needed a door, and we made it a door of ivory with the double blank of the dominoes, and a portico of three cigarettes—two for pillars and one to lie on the top of the pillars and complete the portico. You have no idea how fine the whole thing looked—like a strong little house of ebony and ivory—a little sombre in appearance perhaps, and like a house that has a secret to keep, but quite fine. The palm trees we made out of pieces of larch and yew fastened by Plasticine to the tops of elder twigs—and elder twigs have a graceful carriage, not too upright and yet not drooping. They look very like the trunks of tropical trees. But if you have not elders and larches and yew trees to command, you can make trees for your city in other ways. For little trees in tubs we had southernwood stuck in cotton reels—these make enchanting tubs, and there are a good many different shapes, so that your flower tubs are pleasantly varied. Fir cones we found useful, too; they made magnificent *chevaux de frise*.

Larch Palm.

On the first day of building what we soon came to call magic cities we trusted to inspiration; there was no time for thought. And this day was perhaps the most interesting day of all—for we had everything to learn. One of the things which I learned was that this magic city game was an excellent training for eye and hand, as well as for the imagination and the more soothing of the domestic virtues. The eye is trained to perceive likenesses and differences in the shapes and colours of things—to notice, as I said, that a bowl is a dome wrong way up, and that cigarettes are like white pillars. A beautiful yet sinister temple might be built with cigars for pillars and cigar-boxes for pediments, if cigars were the sort of things you were ever allowed to play with. You see that yew and larch and elder can be made to look like palm trees, and that shrubs in tubs are really like sprigs of southernwood in cotton reels. You go about with eyes newly opened to form and colour: you look at every object in a new light, trying to see whether it is or is not like something else—something that can be used in your magic city. You notice that a door is much the same shape as auntie's mother-of-pearl card-case, and your architectural instinct, already beginning to develop, assures you that a pearly door would be a beautiful thing for a temple, if only auntie sees things in the same light as you do. You perceive that a cribbage board is straight and narrow, as a path leading to such a door might be, and that if you stick tiny tufts of southernwood or veronica into the holes along the ivory sides of your path, your path will run between two little green hedges. You will notice that books make colonnades darkly mysterious if the lids of the brick boxes are laid along the back and along the top, and that based on these solidly built colonnades your bricks and arches will rise in galleries of unexpected dignity and charm. The building itself, the placing of bricks and dominoes, and books and chessmen and bowls, with exactness and neatness, is in itself a lesson in firm and delicate handling, such a lesson as is impossible if you are building with bricks alone. The call on the imagination is strong and clear. A house—the meanest hut—cannot be built without a plan or without an architect, though the architect may be only a little child and the plan may be only a little child's dream. To build without a plan is to heap bricks one on another, to make a cairn, not a house. The plan for the magic city, then, gets itself dreamed—the child's imagination learns to know what the bowl will look like when it is upside down, and, presently, what sort of bowls and books and bricks are needed to give to the cloud-capped palace of its desire some shadow in solid fact perceptible to the senses. To create in the image of his dream is the hope and the despair of every artist. And even though the image be distorted—as in all works of art, even the greatest, it always must be—yet it is joy even to have created the poorest image of a dream.

And in the labour of creation will blossom those domestic virtues which best adorn the home; patience—for it is not often that for the young architect dream and image even vaguely coincide at the first effort, or the second or the third; good temper, for no one can build anything in a rage. The spirit of anger is the enemy of the spirit of architecture. And besides, being angry may make your hand shake, and then nothing is any good. Perseverance too, without which patience is a mere passive endurance. All these grow strong while you build your cities and try to make visible your dream.

I do not mean that a child building a city sees all of it at once—in every detail; I don't suppose even the heaviest of architects does that. But I mean that he sees the masses of it with the eye of the mind and arrives by experiment at the details that best suit those masses. If the glass ash-tray will not do, the tea-cup without a handle will—or perhaps the flower-pot saucer, or the lid of a cocoa-tin.... One must look about, and find something that *will* do, something which when it is put in its place will seem the only possible thing. I don't know how real architects work, but this is how you work with magic cities.

The Magic City.

CHAPTER V

MATERIALS

You wander round the house seeking beautiful things which look like other beautiful things. Let us suppose that you have the run of a house where beautiful things are. I will tell you afterwards what to do in the house where beautiful—or at any rate costly—things are not. It is best when the owner of the house is an enthusiastic member of the building party; then she will grudge nothing.

In the drawing-room you will find silver candlesticks and a silver inkstand. The candlesticks are like pillars. Put the inkstand across the pillars and you have a gateway of unexampled splendour. If there be a silver-backed blotting-book, take it. It will make the great door of your greatest temple. Silver bowls should not be passed by, nor bronzes. A vase of Japanese bronze set up between two ebony elephants crowns a flat pillared building with splendour. There may be Chinese dragons or Egyptian gods that have lain a thousand years safe in their bronze amid the sands of the desert, cast aside by the foot of the camel, unseen in the shadow of the tent, and now decking the mantelpiece of the room you are looting. Little silver figures of knights in armour and what not—take them if you get the chance. Chessmen, too, as many as you can get, the carved ivory ones, of red and white, and the black and brown kind where the heads of the kings and queens are so like marbles and those of the pawns like boot-buttons; draughts too, and spillikins, and those little metal animals, heavy and coloured life-like, which you see on glass shelves in the fancy shop: take them too. They will serve other uses than those to which you will dedicate your Noah's Ark animals. Card counters, especially the golden and mother-of-pearl kinds, and dominoes, and the willow-pattern pots and a blue cup or so from the glass-fronted cupboard. Take all these, always giving preference to the things that you will not be asked to put back the same day. Little Japanese cabinets, tea-caddies of tortoiseshell or wood or silver, silver boxes—and boxes of all beautiful kinds. Do not take the playing cards that people play bridge with: these are never quite the same after they have been used in magic cities, and the Queen of Hearts always gets lost. You can usually acquire odd packs of cards that nobody wants. Those with black and gold backs are the best. They make gorgeous pagodas, and a touch of Plasticine keeps each card where it should be.

In the dining-room you may acquire perhaps, at least you can in mine, brass finger-bowls, and the lids of urns and kettles from the dresser—egg-cups and mugs and basins of lustre and of blue. Also those very little pewter liqueur-cups from Liberty's, and the tumblers for your towers of light, if you are going to have any. The library will yield you books and atlases—very useful for roofs these last, if they do not slope too much from back to edge; if they do, you can get even with them by wedges of paper laid in on the thin side.

But the kitchen will be your happiest hunting-ground, and here you will make a good bag even in those houses where you are not allowed any of the treasures from the drawing-room or the dining-room.

Tins—tins of all kinds and shapes, from the tin that once held Bath Olivers and its lesser brother where coffee once lived to the square smaller tins designed for cocoa, mustard, pepper, and so forth.

Honesty Pillars.

A flour-dredger and a pepper-pot, a potato-cutter, patty pans, and those little tall tins that you bake castle puddings in, the round wooden moulds with which dairy-maids imprint cows and swans upon pats of butter, the kitchen mortar, especially the big marble one, so heavy that cook does not care to use it, brown earthenware bowls and stewing-pots, the lids of tea-pots, clothes-pegs, jars that have held ginger, and jars that have held jam—especially the brownish corrugated kind of jar—all these things and many more you may glean in a kitchen whose Queen is kind.

One of the most beautiful buildings I have ever made was built of kitchen things, and bricks and the boxes of bricks, a few shells, and a few chessmen.

The three tall towers are two cocoa tins and a Bath Oliver tin, very brightly polished; the windows and doors and crenellations are of black *passe-partout,* that nice gummed paper which you buy in reels for binding pictures and glass together when you don't want to have picture-frames. On the tops of the tins are the lids of a silver urn, a silver butter dish, and a silver jam-jar. A salt-cellar (wrong way up, with a white chess knight on it) and a pepper-pot with *passe-partout* doors and windows stand at the base of the tower, and turrets are made of round bricks and draughts, with the chess castles on the top. The porch is a big potato-cutter, with a white chess king on it, and on each side two books with a binding of white and pale gold. Along the top of the porch run the lids of two domino-boxes; on these are two rounds that happened when the arches were being cut out. On these little pearl shells are glued, and little roofs of blue tiles complete the porch. Behind these more books, white and pale gold with marbled sides, lead up to the platform on which the great tin towers rise up against the snowy background (linen sheets over the backs of chairs). The lower building is of the boxes of bricks faced with bricks and bearing a large blue jar crowned with a silver egg-cup, a flour-dredger, and a pepper-pot, and some blue and white tiles. An Egyptian god stands at the corner of the upper and the lower building, and two green trees with white roses grow out of a tomb at the left. The pathway is of tiles edged with fir cones, and two rose-trees within tubs (cotton reels) stand at its beginning; the whole thing was blue and silver and black, and I wish I could show you a coloured picture of it, or, better still, build the thing up for you to see.

The lower platform on the right is a box faced with silver seed-vessels of honesty, and the arches and court are red. The steps are made of blocks of sugar. The tank is edged with red bricks and the water where the seal swims is silver paper. In front is a pavement made of mother-of-pearl card counters, and the inside of the court is made of one large red tile with a pattern of white on it. (You can do this with a square board painted red, and counters laid on it.) The fountain in the middle is a brass match-box and the waters that rise from it are silver paper; but in the picture the water of the fountain seems to have been blown aside by the wind, which no doubt is severe in "those desolate regions of snow." You can build just such another tower and castle with the things you have, but when once you start building you will most likely think of some other way, quite different from mine, and just as good.

Tiles, by the way, are most useful, and if you have an uncle who is an architect he will have any number sent to him as samples, and he will be rather glad to get rid of them. If your uncles are all eminent in other walks of life it is a pity, but you are probably friends with the man who papers and paints your house, or the man who comes when the pipes burst at Christmas, or the man who comes about the gas, or the man who knows all the sullen secrets of the kitchen range. It will be strange if none of these can get you a few coloured tiles when once they know you want them. It is well, if you are a child with a taste for building, to take pains to become acquainted with all the men who come to your house to do interesting things with tools and wood and iron and lead. Quite apart from the joy of watching their slow and mysterious processes, and thinking how easy it would be to be a plumber or a paperhanger yourself, there are all sorts of things left over from their work which are of no use to them, but may be of much use to you. All sorts of screws and nails, for instance, these generous men will now and then bestow—little screws of dry colour, little pieces of brass, door-knobs and finger-plates, thick red earthenware pipe, good for towers, lengths of pleasantly coloured wall-paper—the wrong side of which, being plain, can be used for all sorts of purposes. Lead piping is useful too, especially if you get it cut into 2-in. lengths—and cut *straight*. The sections make excellent and stable flower-pots for cities. Bits of brass tubing are useful too—in fact, brass objects of all sorts deserve your careful consideration. Because, if a city is to look handsome, it must have a good deal of metal about it, as the cities in Atlantis did.

As I write I see more and more clearly that a sharp distinction must be drawn between cities built and demolished in an afternoon, and cities that can be kept going and added to day by day for weeks. You may often be fortunate enough to raid drawing-room and dining-room and to use the spoils for a building that only lasts a day, but no one will strip her rooms of all the pretty things you want and let you keep them for weeks. Therefore if you are going to build a city that is to go on, you must collect the materials of your own, and the odds and ends that amiable workmen will readily give you will take a useful place in your collection. If you let it be known that you want odds and ends of pretty and simple shapes, your friends will save them for you, and you will gradually amass the things you need. I know well enough that there will have to be a place to keep them, but the toy-cupboard, if you clear out all the toys you never play with, will hold a good deal, and many of the things you collect will do for other purposes as well as for the building of cities.

CHAPTER VI

COLLECTIONS

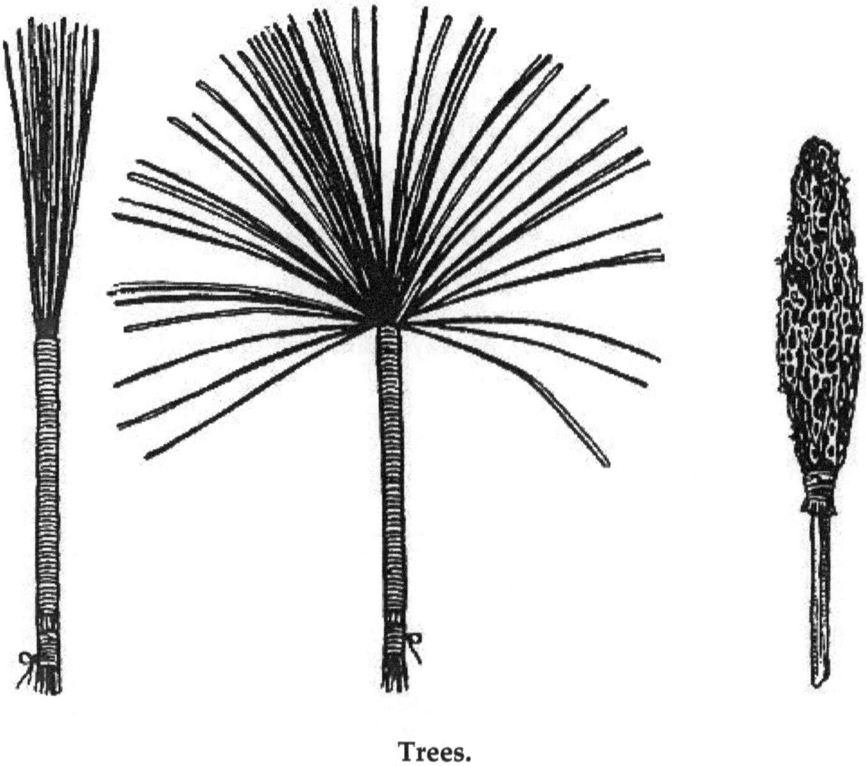

Trees.

First in your building collection will be the boxes, arches, and steps of which I have spoken. Dominoes and draughts and chessmen you probably have. Odd chessmen—quite beautiful ones can often be bought for a few pence—are very valuable for our purpose. The black and red halma men are very useful too, but the yellow and green always look cheap and nasty. Card counters are useful, and so is silver paper. Glass drops off old chandeliers are good for fountains, and pieces of green cloth for grass plots. The back of green wall-paper does for this, too; and very realistic grass lawns can be made by chopping up the long green grass that people sell for fire screens. It is really sedge finely split up, and dyed. You cut it up as finely as you can with scissors, and when you have about a teacupful you take a square of stiff cardboard and cover it all over with glue; then quickly, before the glue has time to cool, you sprinkle your chopped grass thickly all over it and leave it to dry. Next day, *not before,* spread a newspaper and turn the cardboard over so that the loose grass falls away on to the paper. Fasten down your grass plot in a suitable place in your city and build a little red brick wall round it with a little arched gateway, and you will have a neat and charming enclosed garden. For garden beds dark-coloured tobacco makes good mould, and shows up your little rose-trees. You can make standard rose-trees of loofah—dyed green, and the stalks of long matches painted brown. The roses, which are stuck on with glue, are red or white immortelles, and the whole effect is just what you are trying for. Large trees can be made of sprigs of box or veronica, with immortelles glued on, and they will last fresh and pretty about a week. Palm trees can be made of elder stems and larch or of the sedge grass.

Lay the grass evenly and, beginning about half-way down, wind brown wool or silk thread round and round closely and, very like splicing a cricket bat, work downwards towards the thick part of the grass stalk. Fasten the end very strongly. Then stick the stem in a cotton reel or a lead piping pot, cut off, evenly, the loose ends of the grass, fold them back level, cut the stem.

For the city of a day sprigs of southernwood, lavender, thyme, or marjoram make charming little trees.

Shells are extremely useful for decoration and produce the effect of carving. Almost all shells will be useful in one way or another, but I have found the most satisfaction in the gray and pearly shells which you find among the thick seaweed ridges on the beach below the grey cliffs of Cornwall, and the little yellow periwinkly shells that lie on the rocks below the white cliffs of Kent. If you glue these shells strongly on arches and pillars you will find them very handsome adornments.

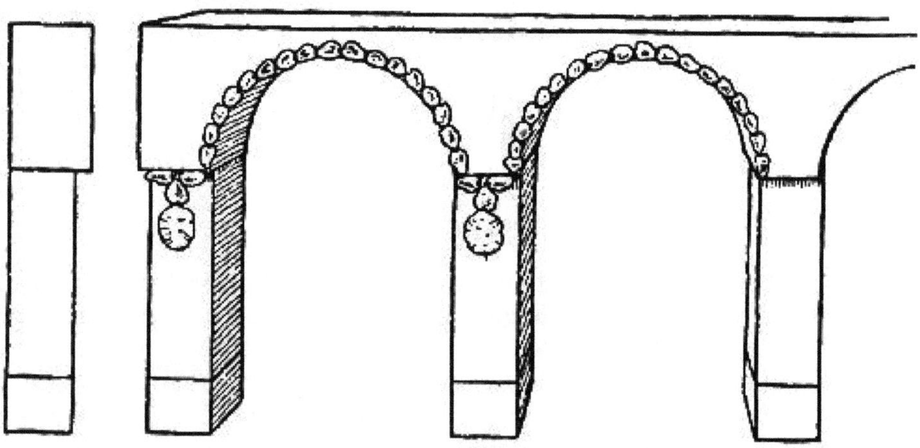

Thick Arches.

Keep your shells in boxes. There are always plenty of boxes in the world, and if not boxes, little bags will do to hold the different kinds of shells. It is well worth while to keep the different kinds separate. The work of sorting out the shells is very damping to the eager enthusiast anxious to execute a decorative design. Indeed, it is well to keep all your building materials sorted each according to its kind, the wooden things together and the metal things and, above all, the crockery things. Keep the Noah's Ark animals in their Ark, and the bricks in their boxes, and when you are going to build don't get everything out at once and make a rubbish heap of it on the floor.

Fan Window.

As you grow more accustomed to building, you will find that sometimes you build a temple or palace that charms you so much that you wish to build it again; and you will soon learn what are the materials needed, and just take out those and a few more from your store. I say a few more, because you will never build your temple or your palace twice *exactly* the same: you are sure to think of some improvement, however small.

I have made beautiful windows with the sticks of an old ivory fan, framed in dark wood bricks, and ornamented the dark wall above with elephant tusk shells and others, and below with carved ivory card counters.

The Elephant Temple.

There is a certain Elephant Temple which I have built many times. Its floor is a red and white chessboard, and its roof is supported on a double row of white pillars. White pillars surround the altar—a wooden box—on which the ebony elephant stands. On each side of him are red fairy lights, hidden by buttresses from the human eye which peeps through the brazen gates into that shadowy interior, and falling full on the elephant on his pillared shrine. The walls are of big red books—*Sheridan's Plays*, *Tom Jones*, and Boswell's *Life of Johnson*. The roof is a flat square lid, once the lid of a packing case, stained a dark brown like the bricks. On the side are the windows made of the ivory fan, and the dark bricks and the elephant tusk shells. There is a door, too, a mother-of-pearl one; in a former life it was the card-case of a much-loved aunt, who nobly contributed it to the Temple. Above this door is a white animal from the Noah's Ark.

And all the rest of that wall is built up of dark-stained brown wooden bricks. The other side shows between dark buttresses the red of the books, and towards the back of this side are small square buildings—wooden boxes stained brown—with brass domes and mysterious doorways. I think the priests and attendants of the Temple live here.

The front of the Temple shows a little of the red between dark buttresses, which, here, are ornamented with delicate dark carved chessmen. The gate is of pierced brass—two finger-plates for a door, and the brazen pillars of the portico are two candlesticks, which support a brass inkstand, on which stand two yellowish wooden chessmen. On the middle of the roof is a big lacquered wooden bowl—the kind that nice grocers put in their windows full of prunes or coffee. Above is a brass rose-bowl, on that a finger-bowl of inlaid brass, crowned with a black chess king. There are two dark arches with bed-knobs on them, and round the roof are various towers and turrets, and tall minarets made of dark bricks with chessmen on the top.

In front of the pillars at the gate two black elephants stand on wooden plinths, and the fore-court of the Temple and the space at the side are paved with mother-of-pearl.

I know the main things that are needed for this Temple, but its details are changed a little every time I build it.

If you cannot get mother-of-pearl card counters you can make a beautiful pavement by pasting the shining pods of honesty in a pattern on a piece of dark brown cardboard, or dark brown paper pasted on cardboard; but if you do this you must build a little dark-wood brick wall all round to hide the brown paper edges. Build gatehouses in your wall, little ones, to show off, by contrast, the massive splendour of your Temple. These honesty pods are a most useful substitute for mother-of-pearl. You can paste them on square pillars or on the fronts of boxes (houses I mean) or make sloping roofs of them by sticking them on folded cardboard fastened at the proper angle by tapes glued about a third of the way up. But as a rule sloping roofs are not good in Eastern cities. A grass garden with paths of honesty, or a shell-built fountain basin in the middle, will add a charm to any city square. And by the way, don't be afraid of open spaces. Have as many buildings as you like, and mass them together as you choose, but let there be open spaces. They will be to your building as mounts are to pictures or margins to books. And for frame or binding, let there be a wall all round your city. It gives a neatness and a completeness which enhance a hundred-fold all the qualities your city may possess.

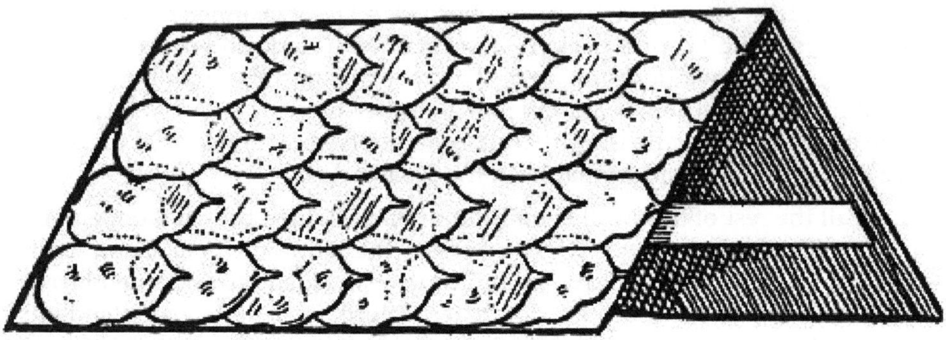

Honesty Roof.

There are cardboard models of St. Paul's Cathedral, the Tower Bridge, and the Temple at Jerusalem. These are interesting in themselves and it is good to put them together. The Temple, which is sold by the Religious Tract Society, is really beautiful, and when you have set it up it looks like a model in ivory. The bridge and the Cathedral are of dull brown pasteboard—but they are interesting for all that. But when you are tired of these things as models, parts of them can be used with great effect in your building, especially if you paint the brown ones with aluminium paint, or even whitewash them.

In the foreground of the picture of the Astrologer's tower you will see a little house which doesn't look as if it belonged where it is. And no more it does. It was put in just to show you what these little cardboard buildings are like—it is one of the gate-houses of the Tower Bridge, and the little white house on the parapet above the steps in the picture of the silver towers is a little gate-house out of another model.

When you are collecting shells, you will find smooth flat stones of pleasing colours. Collect them—the thinner the better—you can make mosaic floors of them, fastening them in their place with glue or a very thin layer of Plasticine. Fir-cones of all shapes and sizes are useful, from the delicate cones of the larch to the great varnished-looking cones that fall from the big pine trees on the Riviera; they call them pineapples there—*pommes-de-pin*—and they use them for lighting fires. But you can use them for the tops of towers.

A little, and only a very little, red tinsel paper is good to use, for the backs of shrines. It gives a suggestion of the glow of hidden lamps—or, put as windows near the tops of towers, it suggests the glow of sunset falling on jewelled casements. You can get it, and also bundles of stamped strips of gold paper, which should be used very sparingly indeed, from Mr. Bousquet, of the Barbican, in London City. There are other things which could serve for part of your collection, but I have told about these in the chapter on poor children's cities, because the poorest child can get them. But they are desirable in any collection, such things as tobacco-tins, jam-jars, clothes-pegs, and the different kinds of common things that you can use for decorating the fronts and backs and sides of houses, if you have not enough bricks to build façades to them all. And remember always to make the backs of your houses as beautiful as the fronts. They may—and should—be plainer but not less beautiful. Do not be like the jerry-builders who spend all their decoration, such as it is, on the flat fronts of their villas, and leave the sides and back flat and ugly, and so that when you see the row of them from the railway they look miserable and dejected, as though they knew how ugly they were and were sorry.

CHAPTER VII

THE POOR CHILD'S CITY

When my city was built at Olympia a great many school-teachers who came to see it told me that they would like to help the children in their schools to build such cities, but that it would not be possible because the children came from poor homes, where there were none of the pretty things—candlesticks, brass bowls, silver ash-trays, chessmen, draughts, well-bound books, and all the rest of it—which I had used to build my city. So then I said I would build a city out of the sort of things that poor children could collect and bring to school. And I did. My friends Mr. Annis and Mr. Taylor, who were helping me to explain the city and show it to visitors, helped me with the building. We did it in a day, and it was very pretty—so pretty that the school-teachers who came to see it asked me to write a book to say how *that* was done. And so I did.

There are no words to express half what I feel about the teachers in our Council Schools, their enthusiasm, their patience, their energy, their devotion. When we think of what the lives of poor children are, of the little they have of the good things of this world, the little chance they have of growing up to any better fate than that of their fathers and mothers, who do the hardest work of all and get the least pay of all those who work for money—when we think how rich people have money to throw away, how their dogs have velvet coats and silver collars, and eat chicken off china, while the little children of the poor live on bread and tea, and wear what they can get—often enough, too little—when we think of all these things, if we can bear to think of them at all, there is not one of us, I suppose, who would not willingly die if by our death we could secure for these children a fairer share of the wealth of England, the richest country in the world. For wealth, by which I mean money, can buy all those things which children ought to have, and which these children do not have—good food, warm clothes, fresh country air, playthings and books, and pictures. Remembering that by far the greater number of children of England have none of these things, you would, I know, gladly die if dying would help. To die for a cause is easy—you leap into the gulf like Curtius, or fall on the spears like Winkelried, or go down with your ship for the honour of your country. To lead a forlorn hope, to try to save one child from fire or water, and die in the attempt—that is easy and glorious. The hard thing to do is to live for your country—to live for its children. And it is this that the teachers in the Council Schools do, year in and year out, with the most unselfish nobility and perseverance. And nobody applauds or makes as much fuss as is made over a boy who saves a drowning kitten. In the face of enormous difficulties and obstacles, exposed to the constant pin-pricks of little worries, kept short of space, short of materials and short of money, yet these teachers go on bravely, not just doing what they are paid to do, but a thousand times more, devoting heart, mind, and soul to their splendid ambition and counting themselves well paid if they can make the world a better and a brighter place for the children they serve. If these children when they grow up shall prove better citizens, kinder fathers, and better, wiser, and nobler than their fathers were, we shall owe all the change and progress to the teachers who are spending their lives to this end.

And this I had to say before I could begin to write about how cities may be built of such materials as poor children can collect and bring to school.

For I have to own that poor children live in such little crowded houses that there is no room for the building of cities, and in the courts and streets where they play they cannot build, for the passers-by would tumble over their cities, and the policemen would call it an obstruction. So if they have a city at all it must be where they have most of their pleasant plays—at school. Besides, the children I have in mind are so very poor, that no one child could possibly collect enough materials for a city. But a number of children could each of them bring a few things, and thus make up enough for the building. And in most schools there will be some children not quite so poor who can afford a penny or so for tinsel paper and the few things—colours, paints, and so on—that do not occur naturally in a house, even a well-to-do house. These, let us hope, will be able to furnish a few old chessmen, for there is nothing like chessmen for giving an air of elegance to domes and minarets. If you cannot get chessmen, small clothes-pegs are good. You can cut them in halves and then you have two kinds of minaret. They can be coloured red or dark brown, or, if your city seems likely to lack metal, you can paint them with gold or aluminium paint. They look well when cut shorter as the battlements of buildings, rather like halma men, but of handsomer and more rotund proportions. Your halma man as you buy him in a box is ever a bit of a starveling. If you cut your peg into three, the middle section will make short round pillars to support little galleries, the roof being a strip of mill-board or the lid of a narrow box.

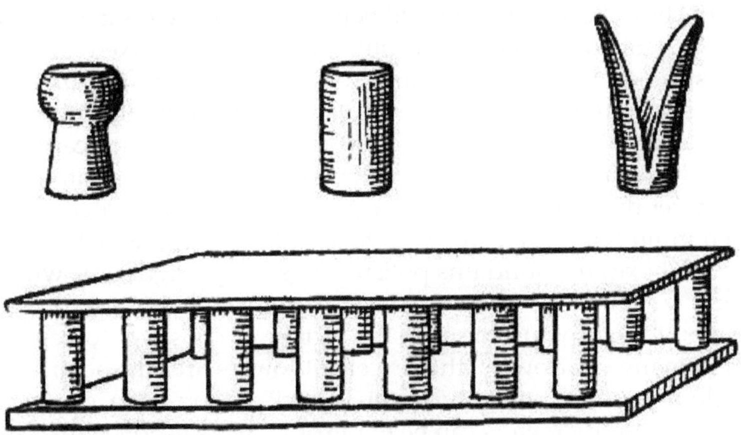

Clothes Pegs.

Towers and Cocoanut Cottage.

Cardboard and wooden boxes of all sizes and shapes are always easy to get. These can be coloured as explained in another chapter, and little doors and windows cut in them. But be sparing of windows; too many windows detract from the dignity of your tower, and make it look like a factory. In poor schools there will not be many bricks, and something must be done to add variety to the façades of buildings when there are not enough bricks to cover or decorate your boxes. A good deal can be done with haricot beans, tapioca, and sago. Fasten the beans round the doorways and the windows with glue or seccotine or Plasticine. If you use glue let the bean-work be quite cold before you do anything else with it. "Next day" is an excellent rule. When the beans are quite firmly fixed, glue the surface all over and sprinkle *thickly* with tapioca so that not a bit of the box shows. Leave the tapioca lying on the surface till *next day*, then turn it up; the loose tapioca will fall off and leave a pleasant rough-cast-looking surface. Round cardboard boxes, such as muff-boxes or biscuit-boxes make splendid towers treated in this way. If you cannot get the little round yellow periwinkly shells, maize is very good if you cut each grain flat with a sharp knife, and fix the grains with glue as pillars and arches. Tin boxes or round tins polished to silvery brightness, with doors and windows and crenellations of black *passe-partout*, can be built into palaces of astonishing splendour, as you can see in the picture of the silver towers. But always beware of too many windows. Other excellent towers are jam-pots: you can paint them any colour you like, but I advise you to stick to terra-cotta, cream colour, and dark brown. Very pretty towers can be made of white jam-pots with windows and doors and crenellation of gold paper. Only you should outline the gold with ink or dark stain to make it show up against the white. Basins that are cracked make good domes, and you can almost always get a cracked basin, however poor you are; tea-cups that have lost their handles, or had a piece bitten out of them, are also not hard to get, and the lids of teapots that are broken, and of saucepans that have been burnt through, come readily enough to the hand of the collector. Honey pots and the little brown jugs that cream is sold in are easy to come by, and make Moorish-looking domes for buildings.

When once you begin to build, you will find that all sorts of things that before looked neither useful nor beautiful become both, when they are built into your city. Look at the bedstead-knobs in the Elephant Temple, and the pepper-pots and the tea-cups on the top of the tower of pearl and red.

Those children who are lucky enough to go into the country for a holiday can collect fir-cones and acorns; nicely shaped bits of wood are more easily come by in a country village than in a London slum. Acorns are most useful, both the acorn and the cup. A brown building with doors and windows outlined in acorn cups with their flat side set on with glue looks like a precious work of carved wood. If you can't get acorn cups, the shells of Barcelona nuts are good, but they are difficult to cut into the needed cup shape. The shells of pea-nuts on a stone-coloured building look like carved stones, but always the nutshell must fit its edges tightly and neatly to the surface and show as a little round neat boss. Your own observation will supply you with other little and valueless things, which will become valuable as soon as you stick them evenly and closely on a foundation of their own colour. The periwinkly shells and the maize grains look best on white wood. The shells of the cocoanut have a value all their own. The larger ones, sawn neatly in halves, make impressive domes for brown buildings, and half a small cocoanut shell will roof a cardboard box that has held elastic bands, and you can call it a thatched cottage or the hut of a savage chief. I called mine Cocoanut Cottage, and the Curator of my Botanical Museum lived there. The Chief Astrologer, of course, lived at the top of his tower, which was a photographic enlarging apparatus. Ponds and rivers can be made with the silver paper that comes off cigarettes, and I have made a very impressive tower with match boxes, painted black and piled one on another so that the blue side shows in front, with a touch of red at each side. Black windows if you like. If you cannot get any chessmen the pinnacles of your buildings must be clothes-pegs, acorns, and fir-cones, with a very occasional piece of lead pencil or short piece of brass tubing with an acorn or a fir-cone on the top. Fir-cones, too, look quite baronial stuck upright on the posts of gates—and they are good edging for paths and roads. Pill-boxes make nice little turrets, and cotton reels, coloured to match the bricks and the boxes, are the finest flower tubs in the world. With sprigs of evergreen stuck in them, or a little made rose-tree, they look quite life-like and convincing, especially if you paste a circle of brown paper on the top of the reel, to look like mould, before you stick your shrub in the hole so conveniently placed in the reel, apparently on purpose to have shrubs planted in it. Cotton reels with acorns or fir-cones on them are good on the top of gate-posts.

Cotton Reels.

These are just a few of the things that poor children can get and the way they can use them. The moment you begin to build you will think of a hundred things that I have not thought of, and a hundred ways of using them that I should not have thought of trying.

If you can so arrange the site of your city that it need not be disturbed, it will grow in beauty day by day, and you will presently have to name a day to satisfy the children who will want to bring their parents to see it. If you give a school party no other attraction will be needed, and you will find that neither children nor parents will tire of examining your city as a whole and in detail, exclaiming at its beauty and marvelling at its ingenuity. And the children will love it. And so will you.

If you are disposed to take a little more trouble with your towers, you can cover them with cement, and mould the crenellations and windows with your fingers. The cement is made of newspaper, size, and whitening. Tear up two newspapers and boil them in four quarts of water for three hours. Then pound the paper in a large mortar, or squeeze it in your hands till it is all pulp. It will have an unpleasing grey colour at this stage, but in the end it will be creamy white. Then add equal quantities of size and whitening and a pinch of yellow ochre, mix thoroughly and let the mixture get cold, when it is ready for use. If it is too thin warm it again, and add more whitening, but do not let the mixture *boil* after the size has been added. When the mixture with which you have covered your tower is dry,—it takes some days—it will be as hard as stone. A cocoa tin set on a treacle tin makes a very neat tower, as you will see by the picture. Square towers can also be made in this way, by covering square tins with the cement. In fact, with a little trouble and some tins of different sizes and shapes you could build a whole palace in this way. Doors can be made of black paper, and lattices of paper cut and folded, with black paper behind it, as you can see for yourself by the picture.

Lattice Windows.

CHAPTER VIII

THE END

You will have noticed that though I began by pointing out that children differ as much as grown-up people do, and that the individual character and temperament of one child are not the character and temperament of another, yet I have throughout spoken of the needs of the child as though the needs of all children were the same. That is because, in the body of this work, I have been dealing with the needs of children as a genus, and not with those of the individual or species. There are certain needs common to all children, needs as universal as the need for food, raiment, warmth, and light. Such are the needs for sympathy and justice, leisure and liberty. These things are admitted by all but the driest economists to be the rights of adults, but not, alas! always admitted as the rights of children. And I have tried to show a little what it is that is essential to the true well-being of all children. The hungers and thirsts of the individual spirit cannot be dealt with by any but those in close relation to the individual child. I have tried to lay down broad outlines—to make suggestions, to point out pleasant ways leading to pleasant places. Parents, teachers, pastors and masters will make the application—or the variation—in every individual case.

One of the things that is the matter with modern education is the absence of the conception of personal idiosyncrasies, tastes, character and temperament. For the matter of that it is this indifference to personality which makes the whole of our civilisation vulgar and vain. Our education treats children as though they were all cast in one mould; it treats men and women as though they, in their sphere, differed not at all one from another. You will say that it is impossible, in a great country and a great school, to find out the personal tastes and wishes, hopes, dreams, powers, and possibilities of individuals, and you are quite right. That is why large schools and large communities fail so detestably in the very objects of their existence. Schools are intended to educate, and they merely instruct. Communities are, at least I suppose they are, intended to enable their members to live happy and useful lives as free citizens, and they only succeed in making slaves of the many and tyrants of the few. The machinery of government and the machinery of so-called education is too big—what it has to deal with is too big—for any fine result to be possible. If we are ever to get out of children, and men and women, anything like the best of which they are capable, we shall have to have much smaller schools and much smaller communities. Some sort of beautiful and useful corporate life is possible in a place the size of Bedford; it is not possible in a place the size of London. Ten or twenty children in a class can be treated as individual human beings, and the best that is in them drawn out by a sympathetic understanding of personal traits and characteristics. But a class of seventy or eighty must be treated as a machine of which the little live units are but wheels and cogs. It can, as a machine, be made to do certain things; the component parts of it can be made to contribute their share to the general result, even as the bright and helpless parts of a machine contribute to its activity. But you can never get out of the children composing such a class anything approaching the fine result which can be achieved by an education based on the broad lines of what is good for *children,* with a superstructure of delicate perception of what is good for the *individual child.* Dick, Tom, and Harry can join in certain lessons and certain games, but there will always be some matters in which Dick is not in the least like Tom, and Harry is quite different from both the others.

The people who govern us talk about education—they talk greatly, and a little they do. But they will not do the one simple, straightforward thing which is as essential to the growth of the mind as vital religion is to the growth of the soul. Any teacher in any elementary school knows what is needed, but those in power do not know it. They will make scholarships as plentiful as blackberries, they will do all sorts of fine things for secondary education. The one thing they will not do is to *reduce the size of the classes* in elementary schools. And so long as this is not done the millions we spend yearly on education are, to a pitiably great extent, millions wasted. We might almost as well take at least half the money, put it in bags, tie it up with red tape, and drop it over London Bridge, or, still better, spend the money in monthly exhibitions of free fireworks, which would at least give the children and the grown-ups one jolly evening in thirty.

A small class can be taught, and taught well, by a teacher of as average ability as ever tumbled head over heels from London to York, but a large class your average teacher will never get at at all. It takes a genius and an orator to speak intelligibly to more than fifteen people. I sometimes wonder if teachers know how much of their teaching their scholars miss altogether—fail to see, fail to grasp, do not know is there. Between the careless or overworked teacher and the timid and rather stupid child there is a great gulf fixed. To such a child the voice of the teacher is the voice of one crying in the wilderness, crying quite aimlessly, in a wilderness of unintelligible jargon. Many boys—in public as well as elementary schools by the way—go through their whole school life "scraping through somehow," and never once having a clear idea of anything that they are doing, hardly ever a glimpse of what anything is about or that anything has any reasonable relation to anything else. It is rather like a miracle, whichever way you take it, but there it is, and a miracle which might be made impossible and unnecessary by a little sensible commonplace legislation. We want smaller classes, and we want those classes better taught. That is to say, we want more teachers, and better-paid teachers; we want our teachers to be placed in a position of certain comfort, that they shall not be living in the House of Poverty with the wolf of Worry always nosing round the door, distracting their attention from what should be their chief thought—for most of the months of the year. We want longer holidays, and a better provision for happiness in those holidays, both for teachers and children. We want every teacher and every child to have a real holiday, not merely an absence from school. In a word, we want more money spent on schools and less on gaols and reformatories. It cannot be put too plainly that the nation which will not pay for her schools must pay for her prisons and asylums. People don't seem to mind so much paying for prisons and workhouses. What they really hate seems to be paying for schools. And yet how well, in the end, such spending would pay us! "There is no darkness but ignorance," and we have now such a chance as has never been the lot of men since Time began, a chance to light enough lamps to dispel that darkness. If only we would take that chance! Even from the meanest point of view we ought to take it. It would be cheaper in the end. Schools are cheaper than prisons.

Now that I have written the words I don't like the look of them; and looking back through this book, I see that most of what I have written applies to the kind of children who are in little danger of going to prison, children in comfortable homes, with enough of, at any rate, material well-being. Most of my book refers to the class that is not taught in Council Schools, and that will not be sent to a reformatory if the eighth commandment is not learnt in one lesson. This class is called the upper middle-class, and it does not go to the Council Schools because it has money to go elsewhere. The children of this class are, in brain and heart, not superior to the children of what are called the working classes. Place the middle-class children in the surroundings of the slum child, and thereupon the middle-class child would grow as the slum child grows, as the plant debarred from light grows—*not straight*. What we want is that there should be a distribution of wealth so changed from the one that now destroys the nation's balance as to put every parent in a position to pay for his child's education, and that the nation's schools should be so superlatively better than all other schools that no parent would dream of sending his child to any school but that provided by the nation for the nation's children.

And now that it comes to good-bye, I am sorry to say it. I feel that I have only been touching the fringe of the greatest problem in the world: that there is very much which I have left unsaid, or which I might have said differently, and better. One might go on for all one's life thinking and writing about children and their needs, and always there would be more unsaid than said, less thought than food for thought. If the thoughts which I have striven to set forth give food for thought in others, if my little candle may help to kindle a great torch, I shall look back on the writing of this book as a great privilege and the memory of the hours spent on it I shall treasure with a glad and grateful heart.

Printed by Libri Plureos GmbH in Hamburg,
Germany

9 789361 381799